PATRICE TSAGUE
MELVIN MOORING

NOTHING BUT A JAR OF OIL

D0111020

seven steps to achieving
financial victory through
BIBLICAL ENTREPRENEURSHIP

NOTHING BUT A JAR OF OIL

ISBN:
978-0-9822237-4-1

LIBRARY OF CONGRESS CONTROL NUMBER:
2009932347

Published by Nehemiah Publishing
Damascus, Maryland, U.S.A.
Printed in The U.S.A.

To contact the authors:

WWW.NEHEMIAHPROJECT.ORG

DEDICATION & ACKNOWLEDGEMENTS
PATRICE TSAGUE

DEDICATION

This book is dedicated to the two women who have had the most impact on my life. My life partner and wife, Gina Tsague, you met me when I had nothing but ideas and visions, you believed in me, affirmed me, and supported me through ups and downs. I thank you for being the first to discover my Jar of Oil. My mother, the Honorable Francoise Foning, you taught me how to make something out of nothing through your example in your business and political life. Thank you for using your Jar of Oil to give me, and so many, a future by your inspirational example and your financial investment.

ACKNOWLEDGEMENTS

Special thanks...

To our chief editor, Julia Nelson, you are amazingly patient and efficient. To all of the copy editors, Kevin Greene, Gloria Shunda, and to all who contributed their testimonies. To the super graphic designer, Henry Teage, thank you for being a creative genius.

To my co-author, Melvin Mooring, and his wife, Beverley Boothe-Mooring, thank you for your continued generosity to so many and your initial investment and faith in this project.

To my church family, Bethel World Outreach Church and Bishop and Lady Chrys Johnson; thank you for your understanding, support and encouragement as I strive to fulfill God's plan for my life.

To my NPIM family, board of directors, advisory board, staff and volunteers, BE teachers, and distributors, Wall Builders and Legacy Partners and all the Biblical Entrepreneurs, thank you for being a part our journey and for contributing to turning our Jar of Oil into financial victory.

To Palm Tree Productions, thank you for being committed to my success and for making sure this project is completed with excellence.

Finally, thank you to the special three ladies in my life, my wife and two daughters Gabrielle and Danielle Tsague; you all make me feel special and significant no matter what my faults. I love you so much. You all mean the world to me.

DEDICATION & ACKNOWLEDGEMENTS
MELVIN MOORING

DEDICATION

This book is dedicated to the two most inspirational women in my life. My mother, the late Odessa Mooring who inspired me to be the best that I could be through God's eyes, and my wife Beverley Boothe-Mooring who allows me to reach further than I ever wished I could, simply because she loves me.

ACKNOWLEDGEMENTS

I would like to thank Julia Nelson who was able to help put into words my thoughts and testimonies.

Thank you to my co-author, Patrice Tsague and his wife, Gina who are so dedicated to teaching entrepreneurship God's way that they were inspired by God with this wonderful message. Thank you for allowing me to be a part of this.

I acknowledge all of the contributors who were so willing to give their testimonies of how God's plan worked for them.

And finally I would like to thank my wife, Beverley Boothe-Mooring. My love, know that all I do and all I am is due to God and His love for us. He allowed us to meet each other over 10 years ago to reach out as one body to touch so many lives, and for you to allow me to dream so that we can see those dreams come true together.

TABLE OF CONTENTS

PART I

7 STEPS TO ACHIEVING YOUR OWN FINANCIAL VICTORY

PART II

TESTIMONIES: HOW 12 BIBLICAL ENTREPRENEURS USED THEIR JARS OF OIL TO ACHIEVE FINANCIAL VICTORY

PART III _____

WORKBOOK

_____

FOREWORD
BY ART ALLY

President and Founder of The Timothy Plan
www.timothyplan.com

There is truth—immutable Biblical truth contained in the pages that follow. Once again, Patrice and Melvin have produced a masterpiece on the Biblical perspective of starting and operating a business.

I believe Patrice offered me the opportunity to write this forward because he knows that we, at the Timothy Plan, not only embrace but actually live by these principles. The bottom line is simply this: following Biblical principles works not only in business but also in every aspect of life and produces lasting success with contentment whereas following secular "business savvy" or worldly principles simply cannot produce the same results over the fullness of time.

As others have shared their business testimonies throughout the pages of this book, I would like to take this opportunity to briefly share two such stories from my life. One is political while the other is directly related to business.

POLITICAL

While I have never had any burning desire to enter the political arena, nevertheless, in the spring of 1990 a small group of us (pro-life, pro-family conservatives) discovered that a very liberal Republican was running unopposed for his fourth term as the state representative from our district. We discovered this exactly one week before the filing deadline and we all started pointing at each other to find one willing to file and run against this guy.

It became obvious that none of the others were going to step up and run so, the day before the filing cut-off, I agreed to try even though I had no money, no experience, no campaign staff, no recognizable name and I was trying to unseat a three-term incumbent! In fact, the only real asset I had is that I believed the Lord was in it and wanted me to run. What I didn't realize at the time was that He didn't want me to win!

Well, to shorten the story, we only had six weeks to mount a campaign in a district that covered three counties in Central Florida. In those six weeks, however, the Lord raised up 150 volunteers (none of whom had ever worked in a political campaign before and most of whom had a two-week family vacation scheduled) and a total war chest of $13,000 to fund our campaign. Despite all that, we did have one distinct advantage – we ran our campaign based on the principles employed by Nehemiah in rebuilding the wall; i.e. every volunteer was to simply concentrate on his or her precinct rather than get intimidated by looking at the size of the entire district.

In the end, we lost the election but won two major victories: (1) In a district that cast several hundred thousand votes, our well-established, well-funded opponent won but he won by only six votes! (2) What the Lord knew and we didn't was that He wanted me to start a Biblically Responsible Mutual Fund Family called the Timothy Plan – which leads into my business testimony.

BUSINESS

In 1992, I was challenged by a Christian CPA friend to start a retirement plan for pastors of independent churches. I got excited about both the ministry and business aspects of the idea and began to assemble such a program. Eventually the Lord convicted me that I could not proceed with the project unless I could find an investment program that engaged in real moral screening. After all, how could I offer a retirement plan – to pastors who preach strong messages on Sunday morning about the evils of abortion, pornography, etc. – that would end up investing their money in companies that were either directly involved in or financially supporting such activity.

To shorten this story also, I discussed my dilemma with Bonnie, my wife and best friend, and we decided that we needed to start a mutual fund family that would employ strict moral screening standards. She even came up with the name, the Timothy Plan, which came from I Timothy 5:8, 22.

I took a leave of absence from my lucrative financial planning practice to perform the necessary R & D. I learned over the two-years it took to put this together that R & D does not mean research and development as much as it means all outgo and no income. During that two-year period, I became immersed in the following:

We appointed the Lord as Chairman of our Board since this was His idea,

- I assembled a pro-forma business plan,
- I drafted a Limited Partnership prospectus,
- I lined up a professional money manager to supervise the funds,
- I located an administration firm to carry out the back office duties,
- And, I started looking for investment capital to carry this project to break-even.

It did not appear to be all that tough, that is, until I encountered a few problems:

- My plan was to raise $1 million and do so by finding 20 solid Christian friends who would be willing to invest $50,000 each. Out of my list of 50 potential candidates, only three were willing to invest.
- The Lord's plan was a little different and He led me to the remaining investors – people I had no way of knowing without His help.

We launched our project as a single fund with zero assets in April 1994, but we had high hopes since we knew the Lord was in this. Apparently no one else knew this because we grew a whole lot slower than what my pro-forma business plan had predicted. As a result, we encountered a few more problems:

- We ran out of money. In our industry, you have to meet strict net-capital requirements or you go out of business. That was the most gut-wrenching period of my life since our partners had trusted me with their capital and it was gone! I had less than a week to raise more capital or close up shop. At the eleventh hour, our Chairman stepped in and provided a way to raise more capital.

- Our growth rate still did not understand my pro-forma plan so we ran out of money again – and again, at the eleventh hour, the Lord brought a new investor through our doors.

- This happened twice more and twice more He brought us new investment capital from sources I had no earthly way of knowing.

I could fill the rest of this book with the numerous miracles He has provided. He has honored us as we have honored Him. We made the commitment one day that we would operate this enterprise based on solid Biblical principles and do so in a Kingdom-Class manner. Our Chairman deserves nothing less.

I hope these two testimonies serve to explain why I love and appreciate Patrice Tsague and Nehemiah Project International Ministries' mission. God has revealed to him and his team a very special insight on how to incorporate His principles into the entrepreneurial world and much of that insight has been incorporated into the pages that follow.

INTRODUCTION

SEVEN STEPS TO FINANCIAL VICTORY
THROUGH BIBLICAL ENTREPRENEURSHIP

Bankruptcy, foreclosures and skyrocketing credit card debt: these are just a few of the financial crises of the new millennium. Unfortunately, believers have not shown any immunity from such ills, even though the Bible provides clear models of, and instructions for, financial victory. Too often, we ask God for a miracle in our finances before we have shown ourselves faithful to follow His Word. Books abound with formulas to "get" God to move financially on your behalf while neglecting biblical principles for creating and stewarding wealth.

Tucked away in 2 Kings 4, we find the story of a widow who obtained the miracle so many of us desire. She went from poverty to prosperity in a very short period of time. Yet her miracle was preceded by remarkable obedience. In this book, we will examine obedience as well as the spiritual and natural principles that lay the foundation for this kind of supernatural intervention of God in our finances.

Too many Christians have defined financial victory as the capacity for unlimited material consumption: you have "made it" when you can buy any car, house or toy you want. This is not what the Bible teaches about monetary success. In this book, we do not characterize financial victory by the size of the bank account but by the state of the heart. A man who can provide for his household with contentment, give to those in need and fund the Great Commission has achieved financial victory. A man who spends millions a year on his own selfish desires is merely a slave to his lusts.

Many believers assume an increase in income would solve all their problems. Yet we have all read stories of famous entertainers or lottery winners who declare bankruptcy after millions or billions have slipped through their fingers. You will learn in this book that industrious and productive work is not something to avoid but to embrace. You will also see that authentic financial victory is always associated with giving to fellow believers in need as well as to the Great Commission.

This book is not a get rich quick scheme or a selection of "declarations" designed to manipulate God. Instead, it offers guidelines to utilize what

God has already given you to be victorious over your finances. These principles transcend time, culture and race. They will show you how to live within your means and expand the Kingdom of God, whatever your income level.

We, the authors, will share our own testimonies of how we overcame significant obstacles as well as the stories of several individuals who have enjoyed successful entrepreneurial ventures after taking the Biblical Entrepreneurship courses. You will hear from a housewife who nearly declared bankruptcy before she was able to start a successful nationwide financial planning business. You will meet a chiropractor who enrolled in a Biblical Entrepreneurship course and upon graduation was able set up her own practice with less than $20,000. Within six years, she had grossed over one million dollars. These stories will not only inspire but also instruct, as they are flesh and blood examples of Biblical Entrepreneurship in action.

So often, we look for an outside solution when God has already given us all we need. The seven principles found in 2 Kings 4 can help anyone achieve financial victory with what he already has. As you read this book, we encourage you to read it with your head and your heart. There are truths within that will transform you as much as they inform you. More than anything, we are confident that as you apply what we have written, you will move closer to fulfilling the will of God for your life and in that, He will be glorified.

PART ONE

SEVEN STEPS TO FINANCIAL VICTORY

Pay your debts and live on the rest

Sell for profit

Trust God

Get Help from others

Block Distractions

Borrow to produce

Assess your Assets

NOTHING BUT A JAR OF OIL

CHAPTER ONE

ASSESS YOUR ASSETS

"So Elisha said to her, 'What shall I do for you? Tell me, what do you have in the house?'"
2 Kings 4:2b

WE have all heard rags to riches stories of people discovering oil in their backyards or winning a talent competition and catapulting to fame. These tales often seem like the exceptions to the rule: we assume that it was the extraordinary individuals or their circumstances that led to such success. Yet in most cases, those individuals merely discovered something they already had. The oil, or coal or gold never moved, but the families may have lived for generations in poverty because they did not realize it was there. The talented individual did not change; others merely discovered what he already had to offer.

Now let us take a first look at our story:

> *"A certain woman of the wives of the sons of the prophets cried out to Elisha, saying, "Your servant my husband is dead, and you know that your servant feared the Lord. And the creditor is coming to take my two sons to be his slaves." So Elisha said to her, "What shall I do for you?* **Tell me, what do you have in the house?"***

> *2 Kings 4:1, 2a*

Here is a widow who is facing financial ruin and the loss of her children to her creditors. Rather than giving up in despair, she turns to the man of God for assistance. Other women of her day might have turned to prostitution, sold their sons without hesitation, or fled from their creditors. Although she obviously predated the New Testament teachings on the obligation of the Body of Christ to women in her situation, she was familiar with Old Testament principles. On at least ten separate occasions in the book of

Deuteronomy, the Lord commands mercy and generosity toward widows and the fatherless. However humiliating it might have been, this widow knew where to go for help with her situation.

Many believers will not go to the Body of Christ with their financial struggles because of pride. They would prefer to take out loans at exorbitant interest rates rather than face the shame of admitting their situation to their pastor or brother and sister in Christ. Perhaps their hearts are resistant to the accountability inherent in such an admission or perhaps they do not have a close enough relationship with a man of God who possesses greater wisdom than they do. Some even follow the pattern of non-believers, filing for bankruptcy to protect themselves from their creditors and "start over." The problem with this strategy is found in Psalm 37:21, "The wicked borrows and does not repay."

Unfortunately, there are cases when individuals do turn to the body of Christ for help but they are either turned away or they receive assistance without accountability, which leads to dependence. When brothers and sisters in need approach Melvin or Patrice, each of them makes it a point to help them take stock of their entire financial situation. What decisions led to the need they are now facing? What can they do to get back on track? Without this kind of relationship and accountability, we will find that our financial problems will continue, even after the immediate crisis has been resolved.

We see that upon hearing the widow's problem, the first thing Elisha asks her to do is assess her assets. "Tell me, what do you have in the house?" he asks her. The term "assets" is greatly misunderstood and yet assets are vital to generating revenue. Briefly, an asset is an item of ownership that can be converted into cash. When assessing our assets, we examine two categories: borrowed assets and wholly-owned assets. Borrowed assets are items that you can legally use, but which have liabilities attached to them. These could include your home, a vehicle, a building, real estate, or even equipment. Wholly-owned assets are just what they sound like: items that you own outright with no debt or payment obligation.

The best assets, of course, are wholly-owned assets. However, there are times when the wholly-owned assets you possess are not enough to generate revenue. This is when it is appropriate to incorporate borrowed assets. We will cover this in greater depth in the next chapter.

ASSESS YOUR ASSETS

Most balance sheets distinguish between "current" assets, which one can convert to cash within twelve months without loss of value, and fixed assets, which are long-term in nature (beyond twelve months). Fixed assets include items such as buildings, land, or intellectual property such as a patent or trademark. Current assets include cash, investments, money that others owe you, pre-paid expenses, and other marketable securities.

Beyond the balance sheet, we must also include the less tangible gifts that God has given us: skills, abilities, ideas, relationships, knowledge, and expertise. Our key to financial victory lies first in accurately assessing what we have and how we can leverage it profitably.

Note also that Elisha did not give the widow money to pay her creditors. So often this is the kind of help we seek when facing financial challenges. We want assistance that will make the immediate problem go away. Yet God is more interested in our long-term growth and maturity than getting us out of our temporary challenges. As we will see, Elisha gives the widow business advice that not only enables her to pay her creditors but also allows her to remain debt free.

Elisha recognized that God has given each of His children something of value, whatever his or her circumstances. As David said in Psalm 37:25, "I have been young, and now am old; Yet I have not seen the righteous forsaken, Nor his descendants begging bread." Elisha's question to the widow was predicated on the assumption that she did indeed have something she could do or sell. Let us look now at the widow's response to Elisha's question. And she said, "Your maidservant has nothing in the house but a jar of oil" 2 Kings 4:2b.

The widow knew what she had, but she did not think it was of any use. Most of us remain in unnecessary financial struggles because we undervalue the assets we already possess. We do not think God can do anything with our abilities or potential. We may even go so far as to break the tenth commandment; coveting what others possess. Instead of looking at what we can do with what we have, we daydream about what we would do if we had a particular skill, ability, as much money as this sister, or if we had the same job as that brother.

When looking at what we currently have, we must remember that God gives each of us talents according to our abilities and the opportunity to prove ourselves faithful stewards. We see this in Jesus' parable of the talents:

> *For the kingdom of heaven is like a man traveling to a far country, who called his own servants and delivered his goods to them. And to one he gave five talents, to another two, and to another one, to each according to his own ability; and immediately he went on a journey. Then he who had received the five talents went and traded with them, and made another five talents. And likewise he who had received two gained two more also. But he who had received one went and dug in the ground, and hid his lord's money.*
>
> Matthew 25:14-18

In the end, the master returns to settle accounts and rewards the two servants who doubled the money. Why was the servant who buried the money condemned as wicked and lazy and cast out of the household? We need to realize that as we demonstrate faithfulness over the assets we have, God will increase them. Yet, like the servant who only received one talent, if we fail to use what He has given us, even what we have will be taken away (Matthew 25:29).

Why did that servant with one talent fail his master? The Bible tells us it was because of fear: "I was afraid, and went and hid your talent in the ground. Look, there you have what is yours" (Matthew 25:25). God has not given us the option to stand still, burying our assets and maintaining the status quo. He commands us to move forward, aggressively investing what He has given us for increase.

We will never learn to leverage our assets toward profit if we cannot accurately assess what we have. Our Biblical Entrepreneurship courses have taught countless individuals how to determine accurately what they possess as well as how the market will receive it. This has enabled many to build businesses that glorify the Lord, provide for their families and expand the Kingdom of God.

The parable of the talents also reminds us that our assets have little value when we hold onto them, but tremendous value when we begin to exchange them. Somebody needs what you have and is willing to pay for it. Your task is to find a way to market what you have so others can make use of it. Do not underestimate humble beginnings. When you first begin trading your assets, you may have to charge very little or even provide your product or service for free. No one may know who you are and you may not have enough experience to command large fees. Yet as you persevere, word will get around. People will see the benefits of what you offer and demand for your product or service will begin to build.

Think about multimillion dollar companies like E-bay, Amazon, or Craig's List. These businesses took off by creating a forum wherein people from all over the world can trade their assets with others. If you believe you have something of value, start making it available to others who need it and let God do the rest. Remember, economic transactions are based on win-win scenarios. A rare book collector may charge top dollars for an old paperback, but he has saved his customers months or years of searching for what they need. What do you have in your house? What can your business supply that others need?

Patrice, who came to the United States at the age of eleven, was not able to complete his college education. Yet after being born-again as a young man, the Lord gave him a simple idea: combine his knowledge of entrepreneurship with his knowledge of the Bible and teach people how to do business using biblical principles. He began training others for free and eventually built a business model to deliver the training to a wider audience. As people followed his instruction, testimonies of success began to pour in. This resulted in Biblical Entrepreneurship (BE), a consulting and book publishing practice targeting Christians who want to incorporate biblical principles into their businesses.

Patrice has gone on to produce books and other training materials and has now conducted Biblical Entrepreneurship courses all over the United States, as well as in other countries around the world. He has certified new leaders to utilize his curriculum and conduct the training in their communities and organizations. He also developed a revenue model that pays teachers for teaching the program and allows individuals to acquire BE distribution agreements for various areas throughout the United States and internationally. BE Distributors have the potential to earn over $100,000.00 a year through the program. On the other hand, Melvin was born in Southeast Washington, DC to a large family of modest means. After his mother died, Melvin's father single-handedly raised him and his eight siblings. Melvin excelled in math and enjoyed serving others, such as running errands for an elderly woman in his neighborhood after school. After earning an athletic scholarship, he graduated from college with a degree in accounting. After growing up in an area that now produces far more high school dropouts than college graduates, Melvin currently has his very own accounting practice as well as multiple real estate holdings. He has been able to use his passion for numbers and his desire to help others to develop a successful career in accounting and to establish several businesses.

What do you have in your house? If you, like the widow, answer "nothing but..." maybe it is time to reassess your assets. Seek the Lord for the wisdom to accurately determine what you have, so you can use it profitably for His glory. If what you have is not enough to bring you financial victory, you may need to borrow other assets. Proceed to the next chapter to learn how.

Chapter Two

Borrow to Produce

"Go, borrow vessels from everywhere, from all your neighbors"
2 Kings 4:3a

At the end of 2008, individuals owed more than $2.6 trillion in total non-mortgage debt.[1] With interest rates often well into double-digits, this has led to stress, bankruptcy, and even marital and health problems. Clearly, debt is a terrible burden to many.

Yet not all debt is bad. In fact, in our story, Elisha instructs the widow to borrow from her neighbors.

> So Elisha said to her, "What shall I do for you? Tell me, what do you have in the house?" And she said, "Your maidservant has nothing in the house but a jar of oil." Then he said, **"Go, borrow vessels from everywhere, from all your neighbors— empty vessels; do not gather just a few. And when you have come in, you shall shut the door behind you and your sons; then pour it into all those vessels, and set aside the full ones."**
> *2 Kings 4:2-4*

It is easy to forget that there are many practices that the Bible forbids in one context, but condones in others. This context relates to the original purpose for which God created the activity. God blesses sex within marriage but condemns it under any other circumstances. The sixth commandment forbids murder but Romans 13 affirms the authority of civil government to wield the sword.

In the same way, while the Bible condemns debt under many circumstances, Elisha actually instructs the widow to borrow containers in 2 Kings 4:3. What was distinct about the widow's circumstances that made it acceptable in God's eyes for her to borrow? We find our first clue in verse four: "then pour it [the oil] into all those vessels."

The widow did not borrow money to buy her sons out of slavery, nor did she borrow money for food. She borrowed containers to store oil, a precious commodity at the time. She borrowed to produce, not to consume. This is the vital distinction.

The moment a young college student arrives in her dormitory or a couple purchases their first home, they will be flooded with offers for credit cards. Our modern consumer-oriented culture has persuaded many people, Christians included, that it is okay to put a new television set, Christmas presents, or even groceries on the credit card. If you see something in the store that you really want, why wait? It is easy to equate "room" on your card with being able to afford that new pair of shoes.

The problem with these purchases is that all of the items you buy will either be gone (groceries) or decrease in value (everything else). None of them will be used to gain income. The widow, as we will see in subsequent chapters, used those vessels to carry and transport a resource to market, which ultimately led to her financial liberation.

Melvin remembers walking into a bank once and waiting in line behind a young man. He was getting ready to obtain a cash advance on a credit card. As Melvin looked over his shoulder at the card, he saw that it was brand new. The young man clearly got the card and activated it expressly for the purpose of withdrawing the cash.

"Excuse me," Melvin said politely to the bank teller who was about to begin his transaction. Then he turned to the young man, "May I ask you what you are doing with that credit card?"

"I'm getting some cash," he replied, a bit embarrassed.

"How much are you getting and what do you need it for?" Melvin asked.

"Groceries. I don't have anything to eat and I won't get paid again for ten days," he explained.

"Let me show you something," Melvin said, pulling out a calculator. Melvin demonstrated to him that at the interest rate of the card and the number of months he was likely to take to pay it off, it would cost him over two thousand dollars to borrow three hundred. The young man's jaw dropped; he could hardly believe what he saw.

"Listen," Melvin said, pulling out his wallet. "Here's three hundred dollars. I would rather give you this money than see you pay that interest. Buy your groceries and cut up that credit card. Don't ever use a card to buy consumable goods again." The young man thanked Melvin in a bit of disbelief, and left. The bank teller could hardly believe her eyes either. Yet that is how strongly Melvin feels about anyone borrowing to consume.

Borrowing to produce is permissible; however, we cannot find any biblical rationale for consumer debt, and thus we conclude that it is sinful behavior. Let's look at the devastation of consumer debt from Art Ally's Biblical Stewardship Series:

- 43% of American families spend more than they earn each year.

- Between 1997 and 2007, credit card debt increased at the rate of $1,202 per second.

- According to a recent survey conducted by CareerBuilder.com:

  - 40% of workers live paycheck to paycheck to make ends meet.

  - 21% of those earning over $100,000 also live paycheck to paycheck.

  - 25% of all workers reported they save nothing each month.

  - 33% do not participate in any retirement programs.

- Personal bankruptcy filings were over 1 million in 2008, the most since laws were rewritten in 2005.

- More people normally file for bankruptcy than graduate from college each year.

- According to The Investment Company Institute, only 40% of US households owned IRA's in 2008 and only 14% of those contributed to any type of IRA in tax year 2007.

Overspending has reached nearly epidemic proportions in our culture.

- According to the U.S. National Debt Clock, the outstanding public debt as of March 11, 2009 was $10,959,059,291,356 and has been increasing by $3.68 billion per day since September 28, 2007!
  - Each citizen's share: $35,837.82
  - Interest on that debt was $451 billion in 2008.
- This year the government will spend more money on interest than on the entire federal budget in 1978.[2]

Furthermore, there are people who borrow to buy items that are permissible in and of themselves—a vehicle or a home, for example— but they purchase a more luxurious car or a larger house than they can comfortably afford. This is also consumer spending because it goes beyond meeting a basic need for transportation and shelter. If your family can live in a three-bedroom house, should you double your mortgage to pay for a five-bedroom house? If a Toyota will get you to work, do you really need a Mercedes? Luxurious purchases are fine for people who can legitimately afford them, but unwise or even sinful for those who cannot.

Borrowing to produce is another matter entirely. Remember that Jesus indirectly affirmed certain kinds of borrowing when He told the parable of the talents in Matthew 25. The master instructed the servant with the one talent that he could have invested it with bankers who would have paid him interest. Even in the ancient world, bankers earned interest by loaning to others. To shun all kinds of borrowing because some debt is bad is throwing the baby out with the bath water, so to speak.

FINANCING WITH A PURPOSE

There are times when you need outside capital in order to grow your business. At the start of your venture, the assets you possess may not be enough to begin generating revenue. For example, if you wish to begin selling ice cream and you do not have a freezer that is large enough to hold it, then your prize-winning family recipe cannot earn any income. You need start-up capital to buy the freezer and perhaps your first month's worth of ingredients. As long as you have done your market research and your business plan is sound, you should be well on your way to paying for your freezer with your profits. To begin, you would combine someone else's assets (the outside capital) with your asset (your recipe) to produce something of value that others are willing to buy.

Sometimes your business will grow to the point where you have maximized all of your assets and once again need outside capital to continue to grow. Let us say that the ice cream business is booming. After nine months, you can no longer fill all the orders from your home. Your business is begging to grow, but you do not have enough money to rent a store location, buy the new equipment to put in it and hire the employees you will need. Again, you will need outside capital to take your business to the next stage of growth. When you understand that this is a biblically permissible time to borrow, you will not hinder your business from growing.

Typically there are two ways to obtain the capital you need. The first is through equity financing. Equity financing allows investors to buy a stake in your business in exchange for the up-front money you need. They will then share in the profits as your business grows and your assets translate into income. The most significant advantage of this approach is that there is no debt to repay; the investors share your risks as well as your earning potential. As long as you are keeping up with your industry and the market remains favorable, you can always raise more money for continued growth when necessary.

The drawback of equity financing, however, is that you must share your profits with the investors in proportion to their investment. Depending on the agreement you reach with them, you may also need to allow them to have input in the decision-making process. Worldwide, this kind of financing has fueled the growth markets in North America, Western Europe and the Far East. Unfortunately, we have found it to be underutilized in underdeveloped countries as well as in struggling communities.

Our primary caution with equity financing is to be very careful about giving up controlling interest in your company. Sometimes, turning decision-making power over to an executive board or a hired CEO can be an exit strategy: you may wish to glean profits from the business but move on to building or leading something else. If you want to stay in charge of your business, you must be very careful to heed the warning in Scripture about being unequally yoked (2 Corinthians 6:14). Do not give people who do not share your biblical convictions decision-making power in your company.

Not every entrepreneur will have relationships with the appropriate people to provide equity financing. Sometimes, even with such relationships, equity financing is still unavailable for a number of reasons. Furthermore, the business may not initially be able to produce enough value to attract equity investors. The second financing option is debt financing. When considering a loan from a financial institution, we must be careful not to borrow too little. What does this mean?

If your new ice cream freezer costs $2500, you need to borrow more than $1000. Borrowing $1000 will only place you in more debt without getting you the freezer you need to store your ice cream and increase your productivity. If you are getting ready to move into your new location, you have to factor in rent, utilities, insurance, equipment, employee compensation, and many other new expenses before your income will actually go up.

Remember that Elisha told the widow not to borrow just a few containers, but to borrow from all her neighbors. He knew she would need a lot for the miracle that was to follow. Although borrowing to produce has its benefits (such as allowing you to remain the sole owner and decision-maker in your company) it also has many disadvantages. Some disadvantages include:

- You are slave to the lender until the debt is repaid
- You must pay back the loan with interest
- You could be forced into bankruptcy by the lender

Scriptural Principles for Borrowing

The Bible speaks very clearly about debt. Even when using debt financing, we must be mindful of these exhortations and principles.

- Proverbs 22: 7 reminds us that the borrower is a slave to the lender. In the case of debt financing, you are choosing temporary bondage for a long-term achievement. When you are in debt to someone, you are under his power. Consider carefully from whom you borrow.

BORROW TO PRODUCE

- Psalm 37:21 tells us that the wicked borrows and does not repay. Bankruptcy and other tactics to avoid repaying debt are immoral. You must be committed to repaying your debt in full.

- Matthew 6:25-34 explains that God knows our needs. He will provide for us without placing us in consumer debt. Even as you consider a business loan, make sure that you are not putting your trust in the loan but in God. The loan is a resource; God is your source.

- 1 Timothy 6:6-7 exhorts us to be content with clothing and shelter. Whenever we spend one dollar above what we can afford, we are being extravagant. Do not borrow for business expenses that can wait just to build an image that the business' revenue cannot maintain. Be content, even in your business operations.

- Romans 13:8 reminds us that we are to owe no one anything except to love him. Pay off your debt as quickly as possible.

- Deuteronomy 28:12 reminds us that we are to be lenders and not borrowers. The goal of every born-again believer should be to walk in covenant with God and receive His promises, including that of debt-free living. Keeping your debts short-term and eliminating them rapidly keeps you as close as possible to God's original plan for His children.

Remember, when you borrow to produce, you are exchanging assets to generate revenue. When you borrow to consume, you are turning assets into expenses. How often do Christians forgo long-term financial victory because of their lust for material possessions that have no lasting value? God is far more interested in our ability to live within our means than in our ability to obtain possessions the world admires. It is better to live modestly and steward your resources wisely than to live a lifestyle that places you in bondage.

As Patrice was developing the Biblical Entrepreneurship program, he borrowed money to publish his books, market the program, and purchase equipment. He raised money from friends and family as well as financing companies. He used his credit card and sometimes made arrangements with vendors to allow him to pay in small increments. This was essential for him and his wife because they did not have any capital when they first started the business.

Patrice and his wife choose to live modestly so that they can invest most of their money into their business and ministry. Like many, however, they made mistakes early in their lives. On one occasion, they attended a sales presentation for a time-share. Of course anyone who has sat through such a presentation knows that this unnecessary purchase is presented as a valuable investment. Unfortunately the Tsagues purchased the time-share believing they could pay it off quickly with income they were anticipating in the near future.

Well, as you can imagine, the anticipated revenue never materialized and the time share became a bondage rather than a blessing. "Unfortunately, we allowed ourselves to be manipulated by a slick salesman," Patrice reflects. "It was a painful lesson to learn, but we are now much more compassionate toward those who have been similarly deceived into foolish purchases." By God's grace, however, they now live with very little debt beyond their mortgage, which they are on pace to pay off decades ahead of schedule. They learned from their negative experience with consumer debt. They now trust God and live well within their means. This financial freedom has allowed them to bless and guide others to the same victory.

---

[1] "Timothy Partners, Ltd., Biblical Stewardship Seminar Series, Revised 2009, Module 2, Page 7."

[2] "Timothy Partners, Ltd., Biblical Stewardship Seminar Series, Revised 2009, Module 2, Page 7 and 8."

CHAPTER THREE

BLOCK OUT ALL DISTRACTIONS

"...you shall shut the door behind you and your sons;"
2 Kings 4:3a

I have only just a minute,
Only sixty seconds in it,
Forced upon me, can't refuse it,
Didn't seek it, didn't choose it.
But, it is up to me to use it.
I must suffer if I lose it.
Give account if I abuse it,
Just a tiny little minute—
But eternity is in it.
—Benjamin E. Mays

DR. Mays, whom we credit with the oft-quoted poem above, knew a little something about the preciousness of time. A noted black scholar and minister during segregation, he would go on to become president of Morehouse College and a mentor to Dr. Martin Luther King, Jr. Later, Dr. Mays would deliver the eulogy at Dr. King's funeral.

The most valuable asset that any of us possesses is time. Every entrepreneur is given the same number of minutes in a day, and an individual's success will be determined by how well he is able to make use of those minutes. Once they are gone, we can never get them back.

Very few entrepreneurs sit around and do nothing. What prevents them from accomplishing their goals is not inaction but distraction.

They sometimes (unknowingly) avoid productivity by engaging in unproductive (or counterproductive) activity. This is especially dangerous when getting a new business off the ground. The prophet Elisha understood this:

> And when you have come in, **you shall shut the door behind you** and your sons; then pour it into all those vessels, and set aside the full ones.
>
> *2 Kings 4:4*

Elisha counseled the widow to block out all the distractions that would prevent her from fully obeying what she had been told. He recognized that the worst thing that the widow could have done would be to deviate from the objectives God had placed before her and thus miss her financial victory. He gave her very practical advice: he instructed her to go into her house and shut the door behind her so that she could focus completely on her new business.

We must implement this principle in our own lives if we are to turn our assets and investment capital into a stream of income. What has been distracting you from using your jar of oil to achieve financial victory?

IDENTIFYING DISTRACTIONS

We can consider a distraction any obstacle that draws attention away from something of priority. If you are a determined person, the devil can probably not convince you very easily to give up on your business. Instead, he will try to keep you busy with less important activities so that your business does not receive your full attention.

To make proper use of our time and guard against distraction, we must be able to identify those things that steal or kill our time. Are there people with whom you spend time who add no value to God's purpose and plan for you life? Maybe they also waste precious hours in the day and encourage you to do so as well. On the other hand, there may be people whom you are called to serve, or who encourage you in what God has called you to do. Time with such individuals is likely time well spent.

Some distractions are so destructive that they will halt you completely from pursuing your goal. Others will merely slow you down. Serious illness, a family tragedy, or a natural disaster can stop you in your tracks.

BLOCK OUT ALL DISTRACTIONS

Yet, if you persevere through the trial, keeping your goals intact, you will soon regain your effectiveness.

The distractions that slow you down are far more dangerous. Pausing your work to watch a television show seems harmless, but if that show consumes the only time you have allotted to finish a particular task you may miss a deadline. A few phone calls, family or household obligations you failed to address proactively, or a disorganized work area are distractions that are far less noticeable than a major crisis. Yet each of these is highly effective in preventing you from achieving your goals. The devil knows that focus is the key to success in almost anything, so he will do anything to break your concentration.

What are the distractions in your life? They could be people or activities. Do you waste time surfing the Internet or talking to people about silly, meaningless topics? Remember to address all your non-business obligations ahead of time so that your work time can be maximized for effectiveness.

James 1:12–15 alerts us to another common source of distraction:

> Blessed is the man who endures temptation; for when he has been approved, he will receive the crown of life which the Lord has promised to those who love Him. Let no one say when he is tempted, "I am tempted by God"; for God cannot be tempted by evil, nor does He Himself tempt anyone. But each one is tempted when he is drawn away by his own desires and enticed. Then, when desire has conceived, it gives birth to sin; and sin, when it is full-grown, brings forth death.

Our sinful and human desires are a prime source of distraction for us in the Christian walk and as Biblical Entrepreneurs. A beautiful woman may turn a man's head as she walks by, while another who is not physically attractive will not. The presence of a woman is not a distraction; it is the man's internal desire which she triggers.

To conquer such distractions, you must address their source directly. What desires are distracting you from effectively utilizing what the Lord has given you? If you are gazing too long at something (or someone) that does not belong to you, then you need to crucify the lust of the eyes. It is best to guard against staring at or thinking too long about something that is forbidden.

31

Do you indulge your body in food or neglect physical fitness? For the Christian it is automatic that alcohol, tobacco, and sex outside of marriage have no place in a life led before God. These habits are rooted in the lust of the flesh. They can distract you from your goals as an entrepreneur because they prevent your body and mind from working to their full capacity. Even addictive behaviors like watching television or playing video games can enslave you if you allow the flesh to supersede the goals of your spirit. Too many people waste countless hours a day on activities which add nothing to their lives.

Many entrepreneurs are also distracted by the pride of life. They make promises on which they cannot deliver to bolster up their egos. They refuse to ask for help or instruction in order to appear like a know-it-all. They begin to view interactions not as opportunities to serve, but rather to be served. They lie and exaggerate in order to solicit admiration from others. Yet they are never the people who will help you utilize the jar of oil God has given you. In fact, they often become a liability in the long run.

"I have often noticed how differently people treat me when they know the degree of financial success I have achieved," Melvin explains. "I have always had a heart to give back to the community, so I have served in many positions that others in my line of work would not. I never make it a point to let on what I do or what I have." Melvin has learned through many different relationships that there are people who will treat him with a great deal of "respect" because of what he has, but he has no use for that kind of admiration.

On the other hand, when an older woman in his old neighborhood died, he made sure she had a funeral fit for any executive or CEO. "That woman helped me buy the first bike I ever owned. I put it on layaway and she gave me the first five dollars even though she didn't have much herself. I wanted that bike so bad, and she helped me get it all those years ago." Melvin, despite his success, has never forgotten where he came from. He has not allowed himself to be distracted by the pride of life.

THE POWER OF FOCUS

Consider a laser beam. The word "laser" is actually an acronym: Light Amplification by Stimulated Emission of Radiation. In layman's terms, ordinary light is concentrated in a very small space which causes it to increase in power. This power allows "light" to cut through metal, perform surgery, and designate military targets miles away. In short, the light is able to accomplish so much because it is focused.

When we focus, we concentrate all our attention and energy on one task. Now that you know what your assets are and you know how to raise the necessary capital to make them productive, you must give the devil no place. You must protect yourself against anything that may draw your attention away from using your assets to generate revenue.

Remember that each of the sources of distraction we mentioned in the last section has a biblical antidote. Do you struggle with a desire for things that do not belong to you? Fight back by being grateful for what you have. Does the lust of the flesh entice you from time to time? Fast regularly according to the Scriptures and keep your body in full submission to the Holy Spirit. Are you tempted by the praise of the crowds and the admiration of people? Humble yourself and God will lift you up.

The journey to being a Biblical Entrepreneur is a serious one. There is no room in God's plan for a short attention span.

> And another also said, "Lord, I will follow You, but let me first go and bid them farewell who are at my house." But Jesus said to him, **"No one, having put his hand to the plow, and looking back, is fit for the kingdom of God."**
>
> *Luke 9:61-62*

God takes our commitments seriously. If we are asking Him to bless our business ventures, we need to take our part seriously. Ultimately, distraction takes the joy out of our journey. Remember that Jesus endured the cross for the joy set before Him (Hebrews 12:2). The key to resisting distractions is to keep our eyes on the prize: fulfilling the will of God and achieving the financial victory He intends for us.

When Patrice and his wife started on their journey to financial freedom through Biblical Entrepreneurship, they were easily distracted. "As we grew," Patrice recalls, "we realized that we were hindered in many of our pursuits because of the time we wasted watching television or socializing unproductively with certain people." Once they realized that those distractions were not going to help them achieve their goals, they learned how to focus on the prize of knowing God and fulfilling His will.

"Television is not always evil in and of itself," Patrice explains, "but it was the devil's tool in our lives to slow us down. We now limit our TV time and are not as easily drawn away by what others are doing. No matter what fellowship activity is going on our primary focus is to finish our work first."

Naturally, the Tsagues have had to be careful not to go to the opposite extreme. At times, friends and family members have expressed that they do not make enough time for them. "We still struggle to balance our obligations to our business and to our friends and extended family. We are persuaded that as the business becomes more stable, we will be able to give more time to the relationships and activities we have sacrificed over the years."

Still, they make every effort not to sacrifice each other and their children: they take at least two family vacations each year, spend weekends together whenever possible, and include the children in business activities. "We have grown to not only enjoy our personal time together but to look forward to it as a break from the business routine. We now realize that we cannot stay focused for long without periods of proper rest, just as the Lord commands."

Just as Patrice had to learn to block out distractions to utilize his jar of oil, so too must all of us focus in order to achieve our goals. Yet the widow shut the door behind her *and* her sons. She did not achieve her goals alone. In the next chapter, we'll learn about the other people God uses to realize His plans for our financial victory.

CHAPTER FOUR

ENLIST THE
HELP
OF OTHERS

*"...you shall shut the door behind you **and your sons**;"*
2 Kings 4:3a

Heav'n forming each on other to depend,
A master, or a servant, or a friend,
Bids each on other for assistance call,
Till one man's weakness grows the strength of all.
—Alexander Pope

HAVE you ever had to stop and ask for directions? Men are notorious for refusing to take this simple step. Even with today's navigation systems, finding your way to a new destination can be very confusing without the help and guidance of someone who has been there before. This is certainly true when starting your own business.

You begin by assessing your assets, formulating your business plan, and if necessary borrowing what you need to get started. Once you have done this, you may find that you still need some help from other people. Perhaps you need some manpower to complete production of your initial inventory. Maybe you need advice regarding your marketing strategy or your industry's insurance requirements. Whatever the need, God will often put people into your life to meet it; however, you must be humble enough to enlist their help.

> *And when you have come in, you shall shut the door behind you and your sons; then pour it into all those vessels, and set aside the full ones.*
>
> *2 Kings 4:4*

NOTHING BUT A JAR OF OIL

The Prophet Elisha knew the widow could not complete the task before her on her own. He instructed her to enlist the assistance of her sons in filling the jars of oil to sell in the market. What if she had disobeyed and insisted on pouring the oil alone? She may not have been strong enough to fill some of the larger vessels or carry them to market for sale. She needed the help of her sons because of the size of the miracle God was about to perform, and because the miracle was as much theirs as hers.

Your friends and family members should understand that when you are blessed, they will be blessed as well. That is why it makes sense to enlist the help of those with whom you are in covenant. If you have not yet achieved your financial victory it may be because you have been ignoring the human resources around you.

Unfortunately, many Biblical Entrepreneurs fail to utilize the wisdom and ability of those the Lord has placed around them. There are several reasons for this:

- **PRIDE.** Sometimes we are too proud to ask others for help. We want to look like we know it all, or we refuse to admit that we are in a state of need. Remember that God resists the proud but gives grace to the humble (James 4:6).

- **FEAR.** Occasionally we may avoid enlisting the help of others because we are afraid of what their responses may be. Perhaps we are afraid that they will not like our business plan, will criticize us for needing help in the first place, or even steal our idea. Relax. If you are working to make your business glorify God, then He will place the right people in your path to help you accomplish it. He will also protect your idea; no one can take from you what God has for you. Remember that God has not given us a spirit of fear (2 Timothy 1:7).

- **IGNORANCE.** There are times when we are not even aware of the talents and abilities those around us possess. Did you realize your first cousin was now an accountant? Didn't you know that the new sister in the choir runs a very successful advertising agency? If we do not take the time to be involved in the lives of our extended family members or get to know those in our church, we may miss out on God's blessing for our lives.

Remember that God lamented that His people were destroyed for a lack of knowledge (Hosea 4:6).

- **BROKEN RELATIONSHIPS.** We must follow Jesus' admonition to stay reconciled with our brothers and sisters. "Therefore if you bring your gift to the altar, and there remember that your brother has something against you, leave your gift there before the altar, and go your way. First be reconciled to your brother, and then come and offer your gift." (Matthew 5:23-24). If we do not heed this advice, we risk burning bridges with the very people God will use to help us in a time of need.

- **INDEPENDENCE.** Many individuals who are known to family members as the "strong one" will hesitate to involve their family when they are going through difficult times. They do not wish to burden those who respect them or rely on them for help with their problems. Yet God strengthens families when they work together through a struggle.

It is tempting to want to shield our family members from any struggles we may experience. I am sure the widow did not want her sons to worry about where their next meal would come from or the fact that they were so close to being sold into slavery. Yet God had ordained that they would be part of the widow's financial victory. Think how much stronger their faith in God must have become; watching the oil supernaturally flow before their own eyes! Involving family members or brothers and sisters in Christ enables them to learn, grow, and experience God's faithfulness along with us.

Remember that God always intends for His children to work inter-dependently. Adam was alone and content in the garden, but God saw fit to make him a helpmeet. Even Jesus built a team of disciples, weak and imperfect though they were, to help Him accomplish His earthly ministry and carry it on after He was gone. Consider the following passages that affirm our need to work together.

> *Two are better than one, because they have a good reward for their labor. For if they fall, one will lift up his companion. But woe to him who is alone when he falls, For he has no one to help him up.*
>
> *Ecclesiastes 4:9-10*

NOTHING BUT A JAR OF OIL

Again I say to you that if two of you agree on earth concerning anything that they ask, it will be done for them by My Father in heaven. For where two or three are gathered together in My name, I am there in the midst of them

Matthew 18:19-20

It is also important to mention, however, that help can be misused and abused. Melvin has experienced this many times in his attempts to serve the Body of Christ. "I remember about five years ago I would take my car in for repair or maintenance to a garage around the corner from my office," Melvin recalls. "I had a chance to speak to the guy at the front desk on those occasions. One day we were discussing the housing market and how difficult it was to get a loan or save the money to purchase a home. He brought up how he and his wife had saved what they thought was enough to purchase a home they had their hearts set on. They actually made it to closing when they were told they needed additional funds."

Melvin is a compassionate man who remembers where he came from. "I asked how much they needed in order to close on the house and offered to loan them the money so they could get their dream home." Naturally, the gentleman was caught between delight and disbelief. He phoned his wife to let her know the great news. Melvin drew up a Promissory Note for the gentleman and his wife to sign.

"In the note, I explained what payment terms that I wanted for the loan. I asked that only half be repaid to me within five years. The other half was a gift from me. They could fully repay me by helping someone else in need when they were on their feet." Unfortunately the couple's gratitude and excitement didn't last long. They moved into their home, but didn't seek to repay their debt quickly.

"In over five years, this couple made only one payment on the loan I gave them," Melvin sighs. "The guy left his job a month after I gave them the loan, so I had no way to get in touch with him." However, Melvin did know the address of the home they purchased. "I found out that they were foreclosed on two years ago. God has his own way of dealing with people. They could have phoned me to work out an arrangement that would have fit them better. Instead, they decided to not repay their debt at all and therefore suffered the consequences."

GETTING HELP

Here are a few things to consider when enlisting the help of others:

1. **Are you ready for their help?** —Sometimes we ask for help prematurely; when we are still trying to figure out what we are doing and have not got the idea or the project to the point where others can contribute. You want to make sure that you have a clear sense of direction and a well thought-out plan before you get others involved. This will ensure that you do not get off track from your original intent.

2. **What type of help do you need?** —You must be very specific about the kind of help you need, because you do not want to get people involved without advancing your goals, nor do you want to waste people's time. Be specific when asking for help.

3. **What type of person are you looking for?** —A well-meaning person can be ill-suited for the kind of help you need. If you have already involved someone you care about, it can be tough to let him go after you realize he is not working out. Make sure you are clear on the type of person you need and do not compromise on your qualifications.

4. **What is in it for them?** —Although most people are generally giving, everyone wants something in return. It could be a simple "thank you," a gift demonstrating your appreciation, or the sense of accomplishment they share with you when the task is completed. It might be something more directly remunerative such as equity stake in the company. Never forget the value provided and remember to reward those you enlist to help.

5. **Who is closest to you?** —Many times you do not have to go far to get help. Your family members, friends, or co-workers could be great resources. You know them already and they know you. All things considered, they will probably be a little more forgiving if something goes wrong.

6. **Who don't you know?** —Starting with those you know is great but don't limit yourself there. The help you need may not come from people within your circle.

NOTHING BUT A JAR OF OIL

"I would never be where I am today without the help of others," Patrice shares gratefully. Patrice learned very early in his journey that he would not reach his full potential on his own. The first person he recruited to assist him was Gina, whom he later married. "My first business was selling women's cosmetics and I figured having a beautiful woman as my partner would go a long way toward demonstrating the value of the products. I invited Gina to a lunch meeting to discuss the opportunity with her, and she agreed. We have been partners ever since!"

Over the years, the Tsagues have been blessed to recruit numerous people to join them on this journey. They began with their close friends; providing them with opportunities to learn to start their own businesses and to be a part of the larger cause of marketplace ministry. Since then, they have worked with many people who came via referrals and other connections. Their organization's non-profit status has also attracted many volunteers. Patrice and Gina are always sure to show appreciation to those who help them through thank-you letters, their annual awards ceremony, and special events throughout the year.

They strongly believe in family-run businesses and believe that God has called each member of their household to participate in what He is building through them. Their two young children are already entrepreneurs in training!

CHAPTER FIVE

TRUST GOD FOR THE SUPERNATURAL

"...and he said to her, 'There is not another vessel.' So the oil ceased."
2 Kings 4:6c

IN April 2003, Natalie, a mother of two, was in a car accident that left her in a coma. Paramedics rushed her to the hospital where doctors worked overtime to stop the internal bleeding. An MRI revealed potentially irreversible brain damage. Her husband, Dewayne, and her daughters, Chelsea and Brittany, prayed for hours for mom to wake up. Days went by with no response.

Natalie remained unconscious for over a week and the doctors told the family frankly that her chances of coming out of the coma were one in a million. Then on Easter morning, ten days after the accident, her family gathered around her to celebrate Jesus' resurrection. As they sang and prayed in her hospital room, she miraculously opened her eyes. Tears streamed down her face as she looked at her loved ones. To the doctors' astonishment, she made a full recovery and is busy being a wife and mom today.

THE ROLE OF MIRACLES

Most believers understand and believe that our God still moves miraculously. Unfortunately, some Christians behave as though God is obligated to perform miracles on our behalf. Particularly when it comes to finances, many individuals neglect what they could be doing in the natural realm as they supposedly wait for God to intervene supernaturally. This is not the role God intends for miracles to play in our lives.

NOTHING BUT A JAR OF OIL

First, we must recognize that God owes us nothing and that any blessings He sends our way are far beyond what we deserve. Second, we should remain mindful that there are believers in need all over the world. In Sudan alone, it is estimated that over 100,000 Christians starve to death every year. How much we have been spared!

While none of us can presume to understand the reasons for such tragedies, they should remind us, at the very minimum, that most of us are already blessed beyond measure. Nonetheless, as a Biblical Entrepreneur there will be times when you will have obeyed all the principles you can obey, and maximized your personal abilities and resources at your disposal. When these efforts are still not enough, it is time to trust God for the supernatural.

In reality, even the best-equipped entrepreneur faces obstacles beyond his control. Market forces change, the economy fluctuates, and prices of raw materials rise and fall. Any of these can have a great or devastating effect on your business. Yet no matter how badly we need the supernatural intervention of God, we are still obligated to do all that His Word dictates as we seek His intervention.

What would we think if Dewayne had not allowed his wife to be taken to the hospital? Suppose he had told the paramedics, "Don't worry. Leave her here on the road. God will do a miracle." We would have thought he was out of his mind, and rightly so. He did all he could in the natural realm, accompanying his wife to the hospital and encouraging the doctors to do everything possible to save his wife's life. When he had come to the end of those options, God sent the miracle.

Let us take a look back at our story:

> *So she went from him and shut the door behind her and her sons, who brought the vessels to her; and she poured it out. Now it came to pass, when the vessels were full, that she said to her son, "Bring me another vessel." And he said to her, "There is not another vessel." So the oil ceased.*
>
> *2 Kings 4:5, 6*

God multiplied the oil to fill every vessel that the widow borrowed. The oil increased in proportion to her faith, which was demonstrated by the number of vessels she borrowed. This widow had a limited amount of oil and needed supernatural increase in order to achieve financial victory.

God met her at the place of her need after she had obeyed His commands and the counsel of His servant. In the same way, Jesus supernaturally multiplied the five loaves and two fish in order to feed five thousand people, with some leftover. God responds to extraordinary circumstances with extraordinary acts.

Furthermore, God does not perform miracles for things we could do ourselves. You would not wake up in the morning and ask God to supernaturally make your bed or sweep your floor. In the same way, you should not expect or ask God to prosper a business that you are not working to make prosperous. Why should He supernaturally send you the customers you need when you have done little or nothing to reach them? Why should He bring you a miraculous discount on your raw materials when you do not even do the research to comparison shop? Never expect God to bring you miraculous success when you are not exhausting every possible option in the natural realm.

KEYS TO THE SUPERNATURAL

Of course there are times when God comes through for us even in our disobedience. These are acts of mercy that we should appreciate deeply. However, this is not a phenomenon we can count on. God warns us that He will have mercy on whomever He chooses whenever He chooses (Romans 9:18). We must never plan to fall short with the expectation that His mercy will compensate for our sin or laziness.

We should also stay mindful of the fact that many unbelievers achieve financial success without receiving any noticeable miracles. As believers, we ask for God's intervention so that He may be glorified in our success. The keys to tapping into God's supernatural assistance are as follows:

- DO YOUR PART —Maximize every opportunity you have in the natural realm. God does not like slothful people. Make sure that you are doing the best you can and trust God for what you cannot do, not what you are unwilling to do. Proverbs 16:9.

- LIVE A HOLY LIFE —Your life must glorify God both openly and secretly or your success will not glorify Him. Ephesians 1:4.

- GIVE FAITHFULLY —Remember Jesus' promise in Luke 6:38, "Give, and it will be given to you: good measure, pressed down, shaken together, and running over will be put into your bosom. For with the same measure that you use, it will be measured back to you." If you do not tithe and give generously as God commands, why would God show you mercy or extend His favor to you?

- PRAY AND FAST —In Matthew 17:21, Jesus explained that there are certain kinds of obstacles that cannot be overcome except by prayer and fasting. These activities bring you to the end of your own strength so that God can show Himself strong to you. There are many great resources to learn more about effective prayer and fasting.

A PERSONAL STORY

Sometimes the miracle you need is not in your circumstance but in a person. Melvin has such a testimony. As a teenager he recalls having a dream of a beautiful young lady wearing braids and a professional, brown suit. He could see her from a meeting he was conducting in a conference room made of glass. Although life would throw him many a curve ball in the intervening time, he carried that dream in his heart for twenty-one years.

By the time of his fortieth birthday he had suffered through a divorce, raised his son by himself, and sent him off to college. "I consider birthdays so special because that is when God decided it was time for us to begin serving Him here on earth," Melvin explains. "Just two weeks earlier I had visited my son with cake and gifts for his birthday. My birthday that year fell on Thanksgiving and I don't recall getting a card or a call from anyone. Here I was at forty, all alone."

For the sake of his son, Melvin had resisted multiple advances from women since his painful divorce. In the midst of his loneliness that day, Melvin did not become bitter but instead turned to God. "As I sat there, eating a turkey sandwich and staring at my reflection in the blank television screen, I realized God did not intend for me to be alone. Even if I found it more comfortable at times, I knew it was not His plan." So Melvin began to pray. He cried out to God for three solid hours, telling God that if He would send the right woman, Melvin would open his heart to her.

Six months later, Melvin was conducting a staff meeting in a conference room. That conference room happened to be enclosed with glass. Through that glass he saw a beautiful lady wearing braids and a professional, brown suit. Melvin recalled his dream immediately and began to lift up a prayer in his heart.

The two met, got to know each other, and that beautiful woman became his wife. "She is the best miracle I could have ever asked for. After years of loneliness, she is the love of my life. God is good," Melvin smiles.

Patrice defines a miracle as a sovereign act of God that provides a tangible benefit to an individual or group for the glory of God. "I have seen the Lord do several miracles along the way which have been critical to my success," he explains. The first miracle Patrice and Gina experienced was their salvation. "I was brought up in a family that was religious but not Christian. I went to Christian school, but I wanted nothing to do with Jesus." Yet God saved Patrice, and three days later Gina also came to the saving knowledge of the Lord Jesus Christ, influenced by his testimony.

The next miracle they experienced was God opening His word to them. "In my early days as a Christian, I used to wonder if there was a special Bible for pastors with more information than mine. I couldn't understand how my pastor could get all of that revelation from a single passage of Scripture. Then God began to show me that the "pastor's Bible" was really His Holy Spirit.

Patrice considers his marriage a miracle as well. "There was no reason why Gina's parents should have consented to our marriage, considering I had only the clothes on my back and a car to my name!" he laughs. Yet God supernaturally opened his future in-laws' eyes to the potential he possessed, and the depth of their daughter's love for him. God continued to show Himself in their lives with the revelation of Biblical Entrepreneurship (BE). "I could never truly claim credit for BE because God gave me the idea and showed me how to develop it. Each step of the way, God has supernaturally placed the right people in my path to bring BE to the next level." A glance at the acknowledgements section of this book reveals just how many people have contributed to Patrice's success.

God also came through with supernatural provision for Patrice, often at just the right time. "I had nothing when I began this journey at the age of eighteen. Yet every time I needed money, God provided through work opportunities or the generosity of others."

What miracles do you believe God for? Do your part by obeying and trusting God to do what only He can do. You are now ready to sell for profit.

CHAPTER SIX

SELL FOR PROFIT

"Then she came and told the man of God. And he said, 'Go sell the oil...'"
2 Kings 4:7b

"You can close more business in two months by becoming interested in other people than you can in two years by trying to get people interested in you."

Dale Carnegie

HAVE you ever been interrupted during dinner by that annoying phone call from a telemarketer, or had a conversation interrupted by someone going door to door? Maybe you just wanted to browse for a new car only to be accosted by an aggressive salesman and forced to sit through a never-ending lecture on how this special deal is only available today. Yet however irritating we may find salesmen at various times of our lives, no one ever succeeded in business without selling something.

As a Biblical Entrepreneur, the keys to your long-term success lie in the quality of your product or service and how well you are able to market and sell it. Unfortunately, many people look down on sales professions. What they do not understand is that all legitimate and honest sales produce win-win situations. You (the salesman) are providing something of value at an amount someone else (the customer) is willing to pay.

No honest salesman can succeed without producing situations that benefit all concerned. If you charged too much, too few people would buy your product. If what you offered was of little value or poor quality, too few people would buy it. When you become profitable after start-up

47

expenses, that is not a signal that you are being greedy. It is a sign that your product or service is worth more to people than the money they have to pay for it. As far as you are concerned, their money is worth enough to pay for your materials and/or effort. Everybody wins.

Elisha instructs the widow in 2 Kings 4:7a to go to the marketplace and sell her oil for profit, "Go sell the oil and pay your debts." She did, and her financial victory came through the sales she made. Remember that even if you have a more traditional job, you are still selling. You are simply selling your talents, time, abilities, and effort to your boss. Selling is the key to any kind of provision.

Start to think of your financial victory in terms of a number of sales. Are you one hundred sales away from your victory? Five hundred? Depending on what you sell, it might only be a few dozen. Here are seven basic principles to keep in mind to help you get there:

1. KNOW YOUR PRODUCT OR SERVICE —You cannot sell something you do not understand. Make sure that you know everything there is to know about what you are selling. Anticipate questions your clients may have and research them. Rehearse your presentation ahead of time so you can easily explain how what you offer can best serve the customer.

2. BELIEVE IN YOUR PRODUCT OR SERVICE —Never sell anything you do not believe in. Customers can tell whether or not you are convinced that what you are selling is of the best quality or offers the best value. If you are certain of the product or service's worth, your confidence will attract the customer naturally.

3. KNOW YOUR CUSTOMER —You need to know what your customers need and want in order to understand how your product or service will meet those needs or desires. Remember, all sales should be win-win. You should be providing something the customer honestly wants for a price that is agreeable to both of you. If you are meeting legitimate needs, you will always have customers.

4. DISCERN THE CUSTOMER'S READINESS —Salesmen become annoying when they try to force a sale. Learn to read the

people you are selling to. Is this the right time? Do they have the money to spare? Are they ready to implement what you have to offer? If the answer is "no" to any of these questions, back off. It is better to keep in touch until the right time than to pressure them when they will say no anyway.

5. CLOSE THE SALE —If you discern that the customer is ready, make sure to close the sale. Many people make a great sales presentation but fail to bring the customer to the point of decision. You may need to stop talking and allow the customer to ask how he or she can get the product or service. At that point, keep the extra talk to a minimum and outline a clear step-by-step process to serve your customer.

6. ASK FOR PAYMENT —Don't forget that the sales transaction is not complete until the customer has paid or made arrangements to pay. Many Christians feel uncomfortable with this step in the sales process. Yet if your product or service has value and meets a clear need in the customer's life, then it is fair and just for him to pay you. Do not beat around the bush, just politely ask for the payment.

7. SHOW APPRECIATION —Once the customer has paid let him know how much you appreciate his business. No one owes us business; we have to earn it. Demonstrate your gratitude in your demeanor, communication, or perhaps through customer appreciation gestures.

All sales transactions should generate what we call Biblical Profit. Biblical Profit is the spiritual and natural gain remaining after all costs are deducted from the gross revenue of the business. Not only does this include income, but also relationships, wisdom, experience, and general goodwill. Unprofitable sales demonstrate poor stewardship. That does not mean that there will not be times to cut your losses: if you baked too many cakes for that festival, you are better off charging half-price at a 10% loss than losing everything you paid in ingredients and labor. Yet the fact remains that without a profit you will not be in business for long. Profit is key to achieving your financial freedom.

Profit does more than generate personal income. It enables you to build a reserve for down times, enhance your product or service, increase your capacity to produce, and most importantly, fulfill God's covenant. Profit is not just something that is coveted by greedy sales people but rather it is an essential part of the ministry of business. Every unprofitable Biblical Entrepreneur will not be able to fulfill God's perfect plan for his or her life. This is why Matthew 25:30 states that the master cast the unprofitable servant into outer darkness where there will be weeping and gnashing of teeth.

How you set your price is essential to selling your product or service. Your price is the amount of money your customer will pay for your product or service. Set your price too high or too low, and you will not make a profit. Consider the following five components when setting your price:

1. YOUR COST —Your cost includes labor plus materials or whatever you pay the wholesaler or manufacturer.

2. WHAT THE COMPETITION IS CHARGING —Before setting your price, you must research your competitors' prices. Your competitors are businesses that provide the same product or services as you provide and serve the people in your target market.

3. WHAT THE CUSTOMER IS WILLING TO SPEND —Equally important to your cost and your competitors' pricing is what your customer is willing to pay for your product or service. You can learn more about this by doing a test marketing promotion with different prices or by conducting a market survey or focus group.

4. YOUR MARK-UP —Ultimately you need to decide how much you should mark-up your products or service in order to cover your operating costs and make a profit. Mark-up is the difference between what the product or service cost you and the price you charge the customer.

5. INTANGIBLE VALUE —Sometimes your product or service provides a benefit to your customers, which is not immediately quantifiable in financial terms. These benefits could include

comfort, peace of mind, spiritual edification, challenge, or inspiration, and they can be calculated into your pricing as well.

Sales came naturally for Patrice before he became a Christian. "I was always interested in reading about the success of entrepreneurs and I devoured sales books like most people devour an exciting novel," he remembers. "These stories helped me realize that many successful entrepreneurs started with nothing but an idea or a product. The key to their successes lay in their abilities to sell that idea or product to others."

After coming to Christ, however, he struggled to sell BE since the product was biblically-based and targeted Christian individuals and churches. "After years of wandering in the desert like the children of Israel, and several encounters with the Lord in prayer, I realized that I was in my current financial situation because I was unwilling to sell what I had for profit. I was keeping my jar of oil locked away in the closet, instead of pouring it into vessels and taking it to market," he explains.

Patrice began to seek God for a system and strategy on how to sell what he had. He developed a price model for the BE training, materials, and his consulting services. He then developed a business model for distributing those courses and services throughout the United States and the world, providing others with the opportunity to sell the product and generate profit.

"This change brought a radical transformation in my life," Patrice recalls. "Before, I depended on major consulting contracts, which was almost like having a job. After those changes, I was able to make my non-profit, Nehemiah Project International Ministries, less dependent on contributions and more self-sustaining. I look forward to the day in the not too distant future when we will be able to use all our contributions to reach underserved populations with the message and methods of Biblical Entrepreneurship."

What do you have in your possession that you can sell for a profit? Your financial victory may be just a few sales transactions away. Keep working toward that goal and you will soon be ready to pay your debt and live on the rest.

NOTHING BUT A JAR OF OIL

CHAPTER SEVEN
PAY YOUR DEBTS
AND LIVE
ON THE REST

"...pay your debt; and you and your sons live on the rest."
2 Kings 4:7b

"If a man has money, it is usually a sign, too, that he knows how to take care of it; don't imagine his money is easy to get simply because he has plenty of it."

Edward W. Howe

YOU are almost there. You have assessed your assets, borrowed necessary start-up capital, and blocked out all distractions. You have enlisted the help of others, trusted God for supernatural assistance, and sold for profit. What is the last step to achieving your financial victory and ensuring that it does not slip away?

The prophet Elisha answered this question in his instruction to the widow.

> Then she came and told the man of God. And he said, "Go, sell the oil and pay your debt; and you and your sons live on the rest."

> *2 Kings 4:7*

This sounds simple enough: repay your creditors first and live on the rest of the money that you make. Although this is the key to financial victory, countless believers fail to put it into practice. Instead, they often upgrade their lifestyles when their income increases. They purchase things they have been wanting for a long time, or they begin to eat out more often, travel more, or enjoy other luxuries to which they feel entitled. There is nothing wrong with these things by themselves, but if you consume them with money that God has given you to pay off your debt, you are playing with fire.

We have achieved financial victory when we have repaid those from whom we borrowed, have enough left to take care of our families, and give to others in need. Do not be like the couple that received the loan from Melvin: they were ungrateful, did not repay the debt and lost the very thing that was so precious to them. Do not let it be said that God blessed you with a profitable business and you did not take the opportunity to achieve financial victory.

If you are determined to stay the course and stop at nothing short of victory, rejoice! You are in good company. Many believers have followed our plan to live financially victorious lives with great success. Melvin recalls one of his favorite testimonies about a warehouse employee in his company: "Carl was head of the warehouse and one of the hardest working men you could ever hope to meet. He was an all around great guy who would do anything for anyone and often did."

The president of the company knew what a treasure Carl was and took care of him throughout the year with bonuses, and even co-signed on a loan or two. Melvin knew that something must be wrong if such a hard working man was still in need of financial help on a regular basis, but he did not investigate or offer unsolicited advice. Then one day Carl approached Melvin to ask for a loan to cover his mortgage payment.

"I gave it to him without hesitation, but with one stipulation," Melvin explains. "I said he must take financial planning classes with me." Carl eagerly agreed. No one had ever offered him this kind of help before. He showed up on time to every class, ready to learn how to reduce and eliminate his debt, as well as how to save and be a blessing to others.

After three intense months of instruction from Melvin, he began following the plan they agreed upon. "I promised him that if he followed this plan over a two-year period he would not only have all of his credit cards paid off, but would also have $15,000 in the bank," Melvin remembers. Carl followed the plan and it worked out just as Melvin had promised. He was able to make improvements to his home and he had enough extra money to begin participating in the 401(k) retirement plan. More importantly, he began to teach others around him to live financially free as well.

PAY YOUR DEBTS AND LIVE ON THE REST

How can you utilize your business to achieve what Carl and so many others have? Here are a few principles to keep in mind.

BUDGET

You must strive to live on no more than 55% of your after tax income. A sound breakdown of your income is as follows:

10% tithe
5 % offering and alms
10 % savings
20% debt or major purchase savings
55% Living expenses

REPAYING YOUR DEBT

The steps to repaying your debt are very simple as well:

1. Develop your debt free plan. You may need to consult someone with experience and expertise to help you do this.

2. Set aside at least 20% of your income toward debt repayment.

3. Make arrangements with your creditors to stick with that percentage.

4. Aggressively pay off the debt with the high interest first. Mortgages and student loans typically have lower interest rates than credit cards. Get rid of your more expensive debt first.

5. Commit all extra money toward debt payments. Every luxury in which you indulge only delays your financial victory.

6. Once a debt is paid off make sure that it is removed from your credit report. This may take repeated phone calls and faxes. Stick with it! It is very important to your long-term financial success.

7. Once your debt is paid, use the 20% you had been allotting to repayment to invest for retirement, save for your children's education or other major purchases.

Ensuring You Stay Debt Free

There are four simple practices that will ensure you remain free of consumer debt.

1. Maintain a 20% savings account for major cash purchases. This can also tide you over if you have an unexpected drop in income.

2. Keep your living expenses at 55%. This will prevent you from living beyond your means.

3. Invest your extra money. Beyond your savings account, make sure you are allowing your extra money to work for you by sound and well-researched biblically responsible investments.

4. Never borrow to consume. Don't fall back into old patterns of buying things you cannot afford.

"Like most people, financial freedom has been a process for my family," Patrice reflects. "We have had to pay off our debts systematically, and make short-term sacrifices for long-term gains. We have a savings plan, live below our means, and continue to rejoice in each step we take toward our goals."

Do you have a financial plan that includes a budget, debt payments and savings? Stick to your plan so you can enjoy the peace that comes with financial freedom. If you are debt free, guard and enjoy your freedom, and help others achieve the same victory.

Now you have learned the principles behind turning your jar of oil into financial victory. The pages that follow contain stories of those who have actually done it. As you read their testimonies, imagine sharing your own in the near future!

Create your own budget sheet, personal balance sheet, and a sheet to track your personal check registry. These are our gift to you, available for download at:

www.NothingButAJarOfOil.com

How 12
BIBLICAL
ENTREPRENEURS
USED THEIR
JARS OF OIL

TO ACHIEVE
FINANCIAL
VICTORY

NOTHING BUT A JAR OF OIL

Chapter Eight
Elizabeth Brooks
Effervesence, LLC

As a young woman, Elizabeth Brooks, an amateur kick-boxer as well as a fitness and body-building competitor, was not someone you wanted to mess with! "I first knew that I had a gift to teach fitness when I attended my first low-impact aerobics class. As the only black woman in the class, I connected naturally with the Haitian instructor. Her energy and teaching style inspired me to get in shape, but also to explore the possibility of teaching."

Not only did Elizabeth enjoy her classes, she excelled. "After a year, my instructor noticed my weight loss and movement improvement. She invited me to participate in my first AAU Team Fitness Competition. I agreed and we won. The victory was invigorating. I had been bitten by the fitness bug and there was no turning back!"

Elizabeth followed her success in the AAU competition by competing as an individual in the National Aerobic Competition. This required a huge level of commitment: she had to go on a strict diet, learn ballet, and complete multiple workouts each day on top of two-hour practice sessions. "This was the hardest work I have ever done," she recalls.

Her success continued, and in the process she met and married her husband, Ricardo. Yet even becoming a mother didn't slow Elizabeth down. "After I had my first child, I got involved in competitive kickboxing," she explains. "I loved the power and aggressiveness of the sport." After years in the competitive fitness world, Elizabeth appreciated the fact that kickboxing was less subjective; performance trumped appearance.

As her personal career wound down, Elizabeth began sharing her passion for fitness with others as a personal trainer. "When I started Effervescence in 1990 I was very happy just teaching classes periodically and training a few clients here and there. My clients loved me and Ricardo constantly asked me if I was doing this as a business or a hobby." Elizabeth resisted Ricardo's hints that she should expand her clientele. She had always thought of her husband as a natural entrepreneur. He had recently taken Patrice's BE course and seemed full of ideas for her, but Elizabeth considered herself more the artistic type. For a long time, the expansion of Effervescence was a touchy subject for the two of them.

Elizabeth was working as a project assistant for a large organization, but she was also raising two children and considered being a wife and mother her top priorities. "I was reluctant to add anything else to my plate for fear that I would lose touch with my family or that they would suffer from not having me around as much," she explains. She also admits that although she realized she had a gift for fitness instruction, fear of failure was also hindering her from advancing the business.

Finally, Ricardo persuaded Elizabeth to take BE as well. The experience proved transformative. "After BE, I realized I was hiding my talents under a bushel. I was no longer content with the little bit of training I was doing here and there. I realized that God had actually been laying plans on my heart for years to expand Effervescence. I finally decided to move forward with them."

As committed believers, the Brooks' knew their success would not come without the help of others in the body of Christ. Although Ricardo had many years of experience as a management consultant to multimillion-dollar corporations and was the managing partner in a number of entrepreneurial businesses, BE and Nehemiah Project also played an integral role in the development of their business. The Brooks' successfully enlisted the help of NPIM to construct their business plan and also received assistance and advice from donors and advisors who were already successful in the field. "Our church family was also extremely supportive of our business and services and used our products consistently," Elizabeth adds.

Upon creating the business plan for the expansion of Effervescence, Ricardo and Elizabeth entered into a formal business partnership, something they had never done before. The partnership has proven to be both fun and challenging. "We both have extremely strong personalities as well as skills and talents that seem to be completely opposite from one another. We have spent many an hour arguing about who should do what, why, and how, but ultimately we have learned that our abilities are complimentary," she explains.

Over the years, the tug-of-war became a truly harmonious partnership. "I matured a great deal during that time," Elizabeth recalls. "I stopped thinking of myself as the one doing all the work as I realized how much God was working through me. I understand now that His grace empowers me to do all that He has called me to do." The couple took the time to define their roles and responsibilities within Effervescence very carefully and found that they were perfectly matched to launch the company to new levels. Effervescence is now a full service biblically-based exercise and fitness education company. It focuses on empowering clients with information that will change their thinking about exercise so that they become better stewards over the bodies God has given them. They offer personal training to individuals, partners and small groups, as well as class instruction for large groups.

After the business plan was complete they still needed to believe God for a smooth transition to a new facility. "The Effervescence Personal Training Studio was an amazing manifestation of God's power in our lives," Elizabeth remembers. "We secured a lease, equipped it beautifully, and organized it with amazing assistance and cooperation from so many organizations. Miraculously, we were able to sustain a large percentage of our previous clientele even in our transitional period. Our reputation of integrity and character helped us maintain about 80% of our customers with almost no gap in training time." Five other trainers now utilize their facility as well.

In addition to services, Effervescence offers a variety of fitness equipment and has produced a line of exercise videos that enable people to maintain their exercise programs in the privacy of their own homes. Although the Brooks' were able to expand Effervescence initially without borrowing any money, they did need to raise money to produce the video series. Ricardo's business background enabled them to draw up the proper paperwork and they were able to pay back all their debts within a year. "We were always aware that the character of our Christian walk was judged by whether or not we maintained our responsibilities toward the debt instruments," Elizabeth explains. "God's supernatural touch was definitely on us during the process. When we originally researched the venture, we were told it would cost us between $20, 000 - $25,000 to produce one video. We did both videos through the grace of God for around $10,000 from beginning to end."

By maintaining good credit terms with their lenders, the Brooks' have been able to establish their company's sound financial standing which offers them flexibility for any future plans. Effervescence has also allowed Elizabeth to fulfill her calling to teach God's people the value of thinking correctly about their responsibilities to maintain their bodies as God's holy temples. With increased revenue from the business, Elizabeth was soon able to leave her outside job. This allows her to dictate her schedule and prioritize her time for her role as a wife and as a mother to their son and daughter.

"Ricardo has always believed that a husband and wife are the ultimate partners in the Kingdom and sees his previous experience as God's way of preparing him to do business with me. We now understand that the better our marriage is, the better our business will be," Elizabeth explains. "I also see how much my life is a witness to my children. As I become a better witness for the Lord Jesus Christ I am able to balance everything that I do, while remembering that my family is my top priority. I can truly tell my children to follow me as I follow Christ."

CHAPTER NINE

BRUCE WOODARD
BSi CONSULTING SERVICES

"MANY accountants, CPAs, and bookkeepers told me that what we're doing couldn't be done. If I had listened to them, instead of God, my wife, and some other trusted advisors, our business would have never become a reality." Meet Bruce Woodard, founder and CEO of BSi Consulting Services.

Unlike the widow in 2 Kings 4, Bruce had not reached the end of his financial rope when he began BSi Consulting Services. On the contrary, he had been operating his own tax and accounting business successfully for over 25 years. As a degreed accountant from the University of South Florida, he was also an Enrolled Agent (EA), which is an IRS designation reserved for the nation's only regulated tax preparers. This meant he could represent clients before the IRS as well as prepare their taxes. He and his wife had two beautiful daughters and life was going well.

"MY PEOPLE ARE DESTROYED FROM A LACK OF KNOWLEDGE"

Instead of a personal need, Bruce identified a need in the business world. For years he worked with small and medium-sized businesses and observed their frustration with taxes, accounting, and finances. Large, wealthy corporations could afford armies of well-paid lawyers and accountants to ensure that they never paid unnecessary fines or got into trouble. Yet time after time, Bruce watched decent people struggle and sometimes fail. Most of these people, he realized, were not paying attention to the financial details of their businesses—they lacked the basic knowledge to even know how to monitor those details. Was there some way to help them?

Bruce assessed his assets and realized that he had a jar of oil to set these businesses free. He had financial expertise, technical know-how, and a desire to help. Instead of just performing a service, one company at a time, Bruce could empower and mobilize hundreds of companies and thousands of individuals to take dominion over their own finances. As he saw the potential of what he was contemplating, he realized it could also serve as a vehicle to provide for his growing daughters, even after his eventual retirement.

While formulating his business and marketing plans, Bruce happened upon Patrice's Biblical Entrepreneurship class. "When I first walked into the Biblical Entrepreneurship I, Principles of Biblical Entrepreneurship (BE I)classroom, I did not know what to expect. I had been a Biblical Entrepreneur for years, but BE I really solidified my understanding that the business belongs to God, not to me. He owns the whole thing: I am really just His steward."

Still, starting BSi was not an easy decision to make. Bruce's original business was going very well, and he had to use his own credit to finance the development of the technology that made his innovative services possible. Yet because he was borrowing to produce, not to consume, he knew it would be worth the risk. Armed with prayer and a business plan, Bruce began to turn his vision into a reality.

There were times of great fatigue and discouragement, when Bruce had to be sure to "shut the door behind him" to block out all distractions. "There were many days when I was discouraged, overwhelmed, and just plain worn out," Bruce recalls. "Yet in the process, I learned to lay the entire business at God's feet and concentrate on building one brick at a time. Focus on the task at hand and before you know it, you will have a wall."

In BE, Bruce had found a continual source of encouragement and extra training. "Practices of Biblical Entrepreneurship, BE II, helped me to outline where God wanted to take our two programs and further develop the vision—which I now understood was God's vision—for the business. The material in Planning a Kingdom Business, BE III, laid the foundation for the implementation of this vision as well as the direction and mission of BSi."

Bruce has found that as he commits his business to prayer, as was emphasized in BE, God is always faithful to lead and provide. Naturally, some obstacles and distractions do not show themselves until a certain point in the business' growth. The more training materials Bruce developed, the more concerned he became about protecting BSi's proprietary information. Yet through prayer and interaction with his fellow Biblical Entrepreneurs, he was able to develop a web-based solution that effectively protected the materials and served his clients even better. He went from having no training videos online to having over fifty, and is now well on his way to two hundred.

"Our corporate Bible verse is Hosea 4:6, 'My people are destroyed from a lack of knowledge,'" Bruce explains. "Our goal, at BSi, is to empower business owners with the knowledge they need to take dominion over their finances and banking functions."

A COMPANY IS BORN

Currently, BSi Consulting offers two services: ACTS and iACTS. ACTS, the Take Charge Accounting and Tax Savings Program, is a unique alternative for small to medium sized business accounting firms/companies that gives the owner complete control over his banking, credits cards, and accounting functions. Bruce has developed a unique technology to handle the daily accounting by marrying online banking to online bookkeeping services. Constant access means that the business owner is able to know what is going on anywhere in the business, including up-to-date profit and loss statements at all times.

iACTS, the Take Charge Personal Financial Program, offers the same benefits to individuals. It gives individuals their first line of defense against identity theft, and provides them with a personal financial statement to help them monitor their spending and income. It also generates a personal financial statement showing all of their assets, liabilities, and net worth. Participants in both programs are given access to BSi's online web-based learning center that provides training on how to use various financial software, as well as helpful articles on tax and financial planning.

Traditional accountants feel threatened by Bruce's new approach to finances. "Many of them have not kept up with technological developments and see our program as a major threat," Bruce explains. "Traditional accountants, CPAs, and bookkeepers do not offer tax or accounting advice. They want to keep the client completely dependent on their services. We want our clients to be educated and we want to work with them as part of their management team to help them be successful in all aspects of their business."

Just a few years into operation, BSi already serves scores of clients all over the nation garnered entirely by word of mouth. Currently, Bruce is focused on training staff, writing procedural manuals, and producing training videos as he prepares himself for the growth to come. At this writing, the company has several large bases of potential clients to whom it will present within the next twelve months. In addition, many financial planners and tax preparation franchise owners are discovering that the ACTS program is perfect for them. Even before any major marketing efforts, referrals continue to pour in.

ON THE HORIZON

Now Bruce sees much farther than the original plan to empower business owners and individuals financially. "BSi will become the platform for marketplace ministry," he explains. He is formulating ways that BSi can point business owners to a deeper relationship with Jesus, as well as having an worldwide impact for God's glory. He sees iACTs, the individual program, helping the Christian community take dominion over its finances. This kind of stability and effectiveness can greatly improve the Christian community's witness and draw many non-Christians toward a meaningful relationship with Jesus.

Although Bruce is a highly motivated individual, he did not build his business alone. "It goes without saying that my wife, Jean, is my biggest supporter and prayer partner. I could not be the man I am nor where I am professionally, or spiritually, without her," Bruce explains. Just as he had hoped, he was able to put his two daughters, Christin and Alicia to work. As part of the business, they also provide him valuable service and even more valuable encouragement. In addition to his family, he mentions clients like Patrice and his advisor and accountability partner, Glenn Repple, who have offered invaluable support, encouragement, and even access to potential customers.

Other associates have been instrumental as well. "Tom Stansbury has given me guidance in the franchising area and helped me to 'think big.' My first two franchisees, George Langdon and Deborah Warringer, have challenged, inspired, and taught me along the way," he reflects.

By all indications, this is just the beginning for Bruce and BSi Consulting. He continues to expand his website, perfect and expand his training materials, and build strategic alliances for marketing. Whatever the future holds, he can face it with the confidence that he has put his "jar of oil" to work according to God's will.

NOTHING BUT A JAR OF OIL

CHAPTER TEN
CRYSTAL LANGDON
CRYSTAL CLEAR FINANCES

"THEY went bankrupt?" Crystal could not believe what she had just heard. Her husband's trucking company had been thriving for years, but their largest client had just gone under. The matter was complicated by the fact that the Langdons had just pulled nearly all their money out of savings to purchase their dream home: a dream home with an adjustable rate mortgage.

"We definitely made a mistake by buying a house we could only afford with the business operating at peak capacity," Crystal explains. Not only was their family's financial future in jeopardy, but they also felt a tremendous sense of obligation to the loyal employees who depended on their paychecks. For an entire year, they put payroll on credit cards while they sought out new business in vain.

"Finally, we had to shut our doors. We were deeply in debt now, and I sought financial planning expertise to help me find the light at the end of the tunnel," she recalls. She was homeschooling her children, and had taken charge of the family finances while her husband struggled to bring in enough money to cover the family bills. To Crystal's dismay, no financial planner would meet with her, explaining that her family's net worth was too low. "The financial industry turned its back on me when I needed it the most."

NOTHING BUT A JAR OF OIL

The Langdons then embarked on a painful seven-year journey to repair their financial situation. "Many weeks it was just macaroni and cheese and a bag of apples," she remembers. "That was our wilderness experience." The family struggled along, and finally saw its balance sheet improve. This time, Crystal found the financial world welcoming her with open arms.

"Now that we had money to invest, everyone wanted to help us," Crystal laughs. The family made sure that they made decisions more prudently this time around, and laid a foundation for a solid financial future. Yet even with the worst behind them, Crystal could not forget the way they were treated when they were at rock bottom. She realized that she, like the widow, had just paid off mountains of debt with little more than a jar of oil. Could she, a stay-at-home mother of three, help others do what she had done?

"For the next five years, I entered into an intense period of education and training. My children enrolled in school, and I focused nearly all my time and attention on becoming a certified financial planner," Crystal explains. There were many late nights and endless hours of studying for various exams. Like the widow, Crystal enlisted the help of her children. "They read me practice questions while I was cooking dinner and helped me memorize information in the aisles at the grocery store."

That did not mean Crystal lacked challenges with balancing home and business life. Like all mothers, she wanted to spend quality time with her children while building her new career. It was hard not to feel guilty when her afternoons were consumed more with studying manuals than baking cookies. Yet she knew her call came from God and that He would grace her family in the process.

"My husband was my biggest cheerleader during that time. Many days he would just speak faith to my discouragement and cast a vision for where I was supposed to take this business which was far beyond what I could see on my own. During that season, our family sacrificed a great deal of my time and energy so I could achieve this goal. Yet my children were old enough to understand that it was our sacrifice, and later it would be our success."

Another set of distractions that Crystal had to block out as she prepared to start her business came from a surprising place: the

Church. "I am sorry to say that there were many Christians I respected who felt I was doing the wrong thing by going into business," she recalls. "A few could not understand how it was possible to work with money without being guilty of serving money over God. Some also felt I was abandoning my family, even though they were supporting me one hundred percent." At the end of the day, Crystal had to thank them for their concern, but ultimately block out their voices as she pursued God's plan for her business.

Despite moments of self-doubt and exhaustion, Crystal achieved her goal. Once she had passed all her tests and was at last licensed in her new industry, she set to work founding Crystal Clear Finances. Out of debt and generating positive cash flow, the Langdon's were able to get the business off the ground with their own capital. Crystal has always been a gifted communicator and so she connected naturally with her clients. In less than six years, her business grew from a little office in her home, to three weekly radio programs, two financial columns and a clientele of over three hundred, and it is still growing.

Although some of her friends still believe that the work she does with money cannot be compatible with a biblical lifestyle, Crystal has found encouragement along the way. She took a BE class when her business was already thriving and was pleasantly surprised.

"When I started BE, I was already pleased with my business' progress. I wasn't really sure what the course could offer me, but I found myself strengthened in my convictions and even sharpened in some of my skills. I learned that the profit I earned was only the fruit of my work, not its reward. I realized to a greater degree that I was the steward of this profit, not the owner."

Although initially Crystal's family was the only support system for her business, she now has a number of mentors who speak into her life regularly. They are financial advisors with greater experience who challenge her thinking, offer advice, and expose her to new ideas. "I believe that if you stop listening, you stop growing. I benefit tremendously from the input of all of these wonderful people."

God has granted Crystal Clear Finances great favor with pulpit endorsements, media opportunities, and a premium office location. Still, most things have come as a result of hard work and day-to-day dedication. Crystal still has to balance the needs of her family with the needs of her business. She has found that prioritizing and staying organized is the key to doing this successfully.

"I take my lunch hour when my children come home from school. This way I get to hear all about their day and still put in the hours I need to with the business," she explains. She has also helped her husband start two additional businesses and passed on her entrepreneurial spirit to her children. "Other mothers pass down family recipes or gardening hints. Those were never my strong areas," Crystal laughs. "But all of my children now know how to make money. They are all entrepreneurs and I am confident that they will be well equipped to take care of themselves in adulthood. That is my gift and inheritance to them."

CHAPTER ELEVEN
JACQUELINE TENNON
INDIGENOUS BEAUTY CONCEPTS

"I guess it was my godmother who inspired the vision for my business," Jacqueline reflects. "She did hair in her own salon that she built in the lower level of her home. I remember watching her and thinking how much I wanted to do the same thing she did when I grew up."

As an adult, Jacquie got her cosmetology license and became a successful hair stylist. She made good money, but for years opted to rent booth space in someone else's shop. It seemed like so much work to open up her own business, besides, she only had a townhome which did not have space for a salon.

Jacquie's godmother remained her role model for many years. She not only placed relaxers in her African American clients' hair, but also offered a variety of press and curl services for those who wanted to avoid chemicals. It was she who taught Jacquie to study a client's natural hair texture to learn what treatments and services would help the long-term health and beauty of the hair. Jacquie always remembered those lessons and put them to good use. She began offering even more innovative natural hair and locking services for women who did not want to rely on chemicals. As one of the few stylists in her area who offered such services, her clientele continued to grow.

As the years went by, Jacquie realized that she was bringing a great deal of business into the salon where she was renting her booth. Maybe it was time to move forward with her original dream, to own a shop like her godmother had. After her market research confirmed that the natural hair trend was on the rise, Jacquie decided to move forward cautiously. She created a business plan describing her vision for the salon and completed a biblical financial stewardship course to help get her personal finances in order. She also completed Patrice's Biblical Entrepreneurship course.

"BE taught me a lot about how to finance the business and really helped me to count the cost of my project. I am very thankful for Patrice's passion for business and his patience with me during my class. After completing BE, I felt equipped to take the calculated risks involved in opening a shop at my own location." When conditions were right, Jacquie sold her townhome and used the proceeds from that sale as a down payment for a single-family home. She then constructed her salon in the lower level of the home. Like the widow, she did have to borrow to produce. It took additional money to make all of the changes that she needed: new flooring, new paint on the walls, as well as some salon furniture and accessories. She was careful to keep her costs within budget so that she could expect to make the money back in a reasonable amount of time.

"My experience in BE was challenging, but it kept me on the straight and narrow path. I stuck to the plan and didn't overspend. In addition, the truth I received in my BE course forced me to confront some issues from my past that were affecting me in ways I didn't realize. There were ways I was thinking and feeling that I had to move beyond before I could accept who I am, as an individual and as a businesswoman."

"I faced enormous distractions in every stage of building my business. It seemed like every time I had to make an important decision, fear and doubt would flood my mind," Jacquie recalls. She also faced her share of outside critics. Although she was happy to provide relaxers for her clients, she herself wore her hair without chemicals. Many people told her she would never make money as a stylist with natural hair. Every time a trusted friend or disgruntled acquaintance spoke against her vision, she had to block it out.

Yet throughout the process, Jacquie learned to trust God more deeply. "Psalm 139:14 states: I will praise thee; for I am fearfully and wonderfully made; marvelous are thy works; and that my soul knoweth right well," she quotes. "That scripture is the rock for my business as well as for me." Ironically, the way Jacquie wore her hair ended up drawing more clients who were seeking a stylist who would use natural methods and products. Jacquie even developed her own line of skin and hair care products for African Americans that she presents to other salons as well as to the public. At this writing, her salon has been open for two years.

"My home-based hair salon is a beautiful and comfortable retreat for clients to come and receive personal hair care and styling. I concentrate on beautifying women and men from the inside out. My salon also distributes a bi-monthly newsletter that provides readers with hair care tips, health information, product knowledge, and pictures of hair styles created from the salon."

Jacquie also found that God sent many people whose help she could enlist in her endeavors. "Ms. Monica Wise, my sister in Christ and friend, has not only been a client, but has coordinated my newsletter and helped me tremendously to grow my business," Jacquie explains. "Ms. Iyana Tennon is my daughter and encourager. She is always in my corner when I need a true friend, and I love her dearly." Jacquie also expresses thanks for her accountant and financial counselor whose guidance enabled her to purchase her first home which made her business possible. She has also enlisted the help of others on her business plan presentations, and for her ongoing training.

In the end, by borrowing to produce, blocking out distractions, and enlisting the help of others, Jacquie has been able to sell her services for profit and give God the glory. "I thank God for His faithfulness. Only He could have brought me to where I am and will continue to take me where I need to go. It's been a long, uphill climb, but when I look back at my life, I can truly say that I am more than a conqueror through Christ Jesus, just as we learned in BE.

"My business continues to improve my personal financial situation because I have products and a service that help my clients maintain healthy hair and a healthy lifestyle. My customer base and product sales are increasing and my average number of customer visits is exceeding what I originally estimated. God is good!"

CHAPTER TWELVE
DR. GAIL DAVIS
DAVIS ENDODONTICS PC

Dr. Gail Davis might not be your favorite person to visit. She is a lovely person and committed believer but she is also a dentist who specializes in root canals! She explains, "I was actually one of the few kids who liked going to my family dentist. Dr. Ferguson always seemed so happy, whistling while he was working. I was fascinated with the creative aspect of keeping people's teeth healthy and beautiful."

When Gail first came to the Washington, DC area she taught as an assistant professor at Howard University's prestigious College of Dentistry. She also practiced part-time in various offices around the metropolitan area. "As a professor, I loved being able to give back to my students, making a difference in their lives and education. The biggest challenge for me was when the students didn't hold up their end of the bargain: when they cheated, cut corners, and still expected good grades."

Dr. Davis' teaching career spanned more than a decade and she was quite content. Yet God allowed her to experience a "wilderness" which disrupted her comfort and revealed that God was requiring more. "God got my attention by showing me that many people I considered as friends did not have my best interests at heart. It was a painful time and I had to trust Him. Each time I walked into the office I began to see that I was working in the devil's playpen. I finally realized that God wanted me to get out of that situation and move out on my own."

Dr. Davis began to consider opening her own practice. "By working in various offices on a part-time basis, I was in and out of a lot of different practices. I thought a good first step might be starting a part-time practice in a specialty group," she explains.

Unfortunately, the specialty group proved to be a nightmare. So many of the healthcare providers seemed consumed by jealously and pride. Dr. Davis found that her colleagues had no problem lying to one another or even stealing from one another. After several instances of betrayal, it became clear that a couple of other dentists were trying to destroy the practice she had set up. "I saw the devil very hard at work," Dr. Davis recalls. "I knew that if I ever tried this again, I would have to control the environment myself."

"Now I knew what worked and what did not work. God was giving me a clearer vision of what my practice should be. God moved me out of that situation and put it on my heart to start my own practice." Dr. Davis had already been following Elisha's advice to live on part of her income and use the rest to pay off her dental school loans, and then build up her savings and investments.

"I really did not have to borrow any money. I had saved up over the eleven-year period I was teaching at Howard so I had a nice little nest egg," Gail explains. She did have to block out her share of distractions, however. Many of her friends spoke words that were unintentionally discouraging. They told her terrible stories about their own practices: the overspending, going deeply into debt, failing to get patients, and the nightmarish experiences with hiring and firing staff.

"I had to block them out and focus on what God wanted me to do," she explains. The Washington metropolitan area offered no cheap real estate, so she also had to trust God for a location. When she finally found one, there was still a lot more work to do. "We started setting up the office and in His timing He brought the right staff. I was able to pay cash for the equipment. Then, I had to trust Him to bring those patients through the door."

Gail quickly learned that if her practice was to grow, her relationship with God would have to grow as well. "When I was interviewing some staff members and I failed to pray about each of them, I made the mistake of hiring two of them. They both quit around the same time and I was left in a desperate position without any help. This time I prayed. God brought a young lady across my path who used to work for me and needed a temporary job. I was able to hire her for a short time until I found the right people. I knew then that I needed a more consistent and powerful prayer life!"

Dr. Davis casually mentioned to a friend, Shirley, that she could use a Christian mentor for the business side of her practice. Shirley introduced her to Patrice, who began to serve as her business coach. "He has been a tremendous blessing to me and my practice. I also took BE which helped me understand more deeply the type of practice God expects me to have. The Bible had come alive to me for the first time in the areas of stewardship and finances."

Through working with Patrice and Nehemiah Project, Gail has found great benefit in being connected with other Biblical Entrepreneurs. "We are all working toward the same goals in showing the world how a Kingdom-minded business looks. It is truly awesome!"

As her practice has grown, God has shown Gail favor with insurance companies, some of which have given her a special compensation schedule to be part of their plan. God has also kept new patients coming through her doors, even in tough financial times. She explains, "I work strictly on referrals because of my specialty. As I treat people the way I want to be treated, and show genuine care and concern for my patients, they in turn refer their friends and family to me. They also tell their doctors wonderful things about my practice and I get more referrals that way. Yet I realize that all I am doing is letting God's light shine through me."

Dr. Davis' practice is now a financial and Kingdom success. She has the financial freedom to pay for everything in cash, and the liberty to honor the Lord in all she does. "Now I feel I can step it up a notch or two in service to the Lord because He has built up my faith and trust in Him. I have seen His faithfulness, making a way out of no way, as He has continued to send patients through my door in these times. He has taken away so many of my initial fears, which allows me to focus on what He wants me to do. Right now, God has called me to be a discussion leader in Bible Study Fellowship on Tuesday evenings. It is a great commitment and a lot of work but it is also a tremendous blessing. I am loving it!"

CHAPTER THIRTEEN
JOE & HOPE ROBINS
FREEDOM HOME CARE

IMAGINE opening your business and working for six months to land your first customer, only to have him die the next day! That is how Joe Robbins' journey as a Biblical Entrepreneur began.

"I definitely started my business with nothing but a jar of oil," Joe reflects. "I had good credit and a small 401(k). That was pretty much it!"

Joe grew up in the south, and was industrious from a young age; he quickly recognized opportunities to earn money. "I collected bottles and cans, cut lawns, and basically did whatever I could to make a dime," he explains. Joe also learned some valuable technical skills as a teenager by befriending the crotchety old man in town whom no one else seemed to like. "Jack scared other kids, but he didn't scare me. He fixed lawn mowers for a living, and I set to work helping him out. Not only did I learn to fix machinery, I traded my time with him to get a riding mower for my budding lawn care business."

Joe entered the Navy out of high school, where he was stationed in California and quickly worked his way up through the ranks of engineers. Although he was not degreed like most of his colleagues, his work ethic and ability to learn quickly allowed him to advance in avionics nonetheless. After retiring, he was able to leverage his skills to obtain an engineering job with United Airlines, something he had always dreamed of.

NOTHING BUT A JAR OF OIL

Life was good, but Joe was drifting from the Lord. He was married, had great career, and plenty of money. Yet two events shook his seemingly solid grip on everything: the terrorist attacks of September 11th and a traumatic divorce.

"9/11 was tough on every American, but as a member of the airline industry and a military man, it affected me a great deal," Joe recalls. "The divorce was terrible, and left me emotionally devastated and financially broke." Joe headed back to rural Georgia to start anew.

"Unfortunately, I realized pretty quickly that I was not going to be able to get the same kind of job there in a small southern town as I had out in California," Joe explains. "On the positive side, though, God brought me my second wife, Hope. We were childhood friends and she had just divorced after fourteen years, like me. She also had two beautiful children whom she adored. I had always wanted children, and after reconnecting with her, I knew God had led me to someone I could partner with for the rest of my life."

Joe also felt the Lord calling him back to a closer relationship with Him, even as He drew Joe to his new wife. Hope's divorce had left her with little financially, as well, but she did have a good job. Joe's research and prayer led him to a business opportunity to care for the elderly in their home. He recalled his childhood days with Jack and thought about how much he would enjoy serving elderly folks who had no children or family members to look after them on a day-to-day basis. After praying together and seeking God's direction, Joe and Hope cashed in his 401(k), joined The Senior's Choice network, and started Freedom Home Care.

"It was very tough at first," Joe remembers. "We had to give our service away for free for many months before we could create a market." Yet as the business struggled, Joe was forced to seek God like he had never done before. God used the start of his new business to drive Joe back into His presence. Even as it gained more paying customers, Joe felt his heart stirred to make his work a ministry to his customers, staff, and the Lord.

"Now we have over 350 clients," Joe explains. "Our business provides the elderly with caregivers who spend as little as an hour or as many as 24 hours a day taking care of their needs; from bathing and grooming to other important tasks they may not be able to do on their own."

"God continued to use the business to fuel my spiritual growth. As Hope and I searched for a church home, we happened to meet a gentleman from Cameroon. He ended up pointing us to Patrice and Biblical Entrepreneurship." Naturally, Hope labored alongside Joe from the beginning. Joe and Hope took BE I and connected with the broader BE network of businesses. Joe was thrilled to find likeminded entrepreneurs who were glorifying God in the way they did business and with the resources they gained.

Although Joe was already doing a lot of what Patrice taught, there was a sense of iron sharpening iron when Patrice did leadership training for Joe's staff. Joe takes staff training very seriously. "In our business, the caregiver is the product. We have to have the best-trained and best-hearted individuals working for us, or we have nothing. Fortunately when you work for the elderly, the quality of your care cannot slip but so much without you hearing about it!" Joe laughs.

Joe also found that connecting with believers in other industries helped him to get better services for himself and for his business. "I hadn't realized the local financial planner was overcharging me for life insurance until I got a much more competitive bid from a fellow BE graduate," Joe explains.

Like the widow, Joe had to fight to remain focused while building the business. "I always want to take care of our staff," Joe explains, "yet I have to remember to keep the customer first. It is easy to get off track because you interact with the staff far more, but God has helped me remain focused on the mission of our business, which is to serve our customers with excellence."

"It was tough for me to listen to the expertise of others at first," Joe admits. "I always had to try it my way first. However, I learned the hard way that the folks at The Senior's Choice network did know what they were doing, and so finally our business was able to implement and benefit from their established systems." More recently, Joe finds great encouragement from his fellow Biblical Entrepreneurs.

"We really do strive to run a Kingdom business at Freedom Home Care," Joe explains. "We pray together in the mornings, and many of our staff members are able to provide very meaningful ministry to our clients, many of whom are so vulnerable. I am always seeking God for wisdom to put the right caregiver with the right client so that everything we do glorifies God."

As Joe and Hope have been faithful to remain focused and build a profitable business, they have seen a significant improvement in their financial situation. Hope has been able to quit her outside job and work for Freedom Home Care as she has long desired. In addition to Hope's two children from her first marriage, she and Joe rejoice over the two children they have together. Joe sums it up by saying, "God has continued to bless us. Like all entrepreneurs, we have taken risks, and found ourselves in some pretty deep waters. Yet in everything we have tried to let the Lord lead us."

CHAPTER FOURTEEN
STEVE SAPPINGTON
TWM GROUP, LLC

CHAT with Steve Sappington about his work experience for a few minutes and it might seem like there is hardly a job in the world he has not tried. He began his sales career at the tender age of twelve. It was hard to find a lot of doors to knock on in rural Oklahoma where he grew up, but he managed to sell personalized Christmas cards to friends and family. After a high school career filled with baseball and basketball, he continued to work his way through college, selling Bibles for the Southwestern Company.

Steve's interests were not restricted to his major in sociology. "I have always been a quick study academically. After graduating from Oklahoma Baptist University, I continued to live in Shawnee and studied jazz guitar." Soon Steve opened a studio, his first entrepreneurial venture, where he taught as many as fifty students a week.

A few years later, Steve moved back to his home town, where he obtained a Master's degree in education and taught public school for seven years. The move enabled him to help his father with the family farm during the summers and came with an unexpected bonus: he met and married his wife. His next entrepreneurial experience came shortly thereafter, when he and his wife purchased a franchise from Success Motivation Institute and sold training and motivation programs for a year. They sold so many programs that they were invited to move to Waco, Texas where SMI headquarters was located. There they sold SMI franchises for the next few years. After moving on from SMI, Steve would spend the next ten years in the financial services industry.

Steve credits his professional success to his wide variety of experiences. "I can communicate comfortably with almost anyone: blue collar mechanics, Ph.Ds, the guy in the corner office, or the guy in the cubicle," Steve explains. His stint at the brokerage firm was so successful that he soon realized he was making more money for the partners than he was able to earn for himself. Furthermore, as a committed Christian, Steve was very aware of the moral aspects of investing, but he was restricted from discussing them with his clients.

Steve prayerfully pondered his situation and embarked on nearly two years of research to determine his options. He knew he had a valuable jar of oil in his skill set, but he needed the right vessels to carry it to market. His search led him to fellow believer, Glenn Repple, and he is now an independent financial advisor with G.A. Repple & Company.

Starting out on their own was definitely an act of faith for Steve and his wife. "When I left my employer, I had over 1300 accounts that I had built up over ten years. But I had a 'non-compete' clause that prevented me from contacting the clients after I left. I told a few beforehand that I was leaving so I was able to fund our living expenses and advertising from the income those clients generated." At the time, the Sappingtons had owned their home for ten years and were able to pull out some of the equity to build their offices as an addition to their house. Working from home enabled Steve to work the long hours necessary in the early stages of the business, while minimizing the disruption to his family life.

Like the widow, Steve faced many distractions and potential obstacles as he built his business. "Of course my former employer did not allow me to transfer all the accounts at once. Transferring them individually created an enormous amount of initial paperwork," he recalls. Steve enlisted the help of others, including his wife, who served as his office assistant. He lists other individuals who helped him along the way in his new book *Today's WORD on Money*™.

In the process of building his venture, Steve realized that he lacked the necessary training in business and entrepreneurship to grow his organization to the next level. That was where BE entered the picture. "BE helped me realize where my weaknesses were, as well as the areas of my business that I had not fully yielded to God," he shares. "I believe that all our success has been due to God's grace, and to the communication and sales abilities that He gave me. Yet we had reached a point where our growth would have been limited if we had not acquired new skills." These skills included writing and executing a business plan, which Steve was able to learn in BE III.

"We now have around 150 clients, many of whom have several accounts with us. We offer traditional stocks, bonds, mutual funds, and managed accounts. However, we specialize in 'alternative investments' so we utilize a number of products like whole life insurance, non-traded real estate investment trusts, oil and gas partnerships, and equipment leasing," Steve explains. Steve also advises many of his clients when they should seek the help of other financial professionals, such as attorneys, CPAs, or Enrolled Agents. As Steve puts it, many of his clients are interested in minimizing their "gifts" to the IRS and maximizing their gifts to the Kingdom and to their family members.

God has been actively at work in the Sappingtons' ventures, but they are most excited about how He has enabled them to bless others. The same man who once helped on the family farm is now able to meet and help people in need all over the world. "Of course our income has increased, but so has our freedom," he points out. "We've been able to travel and share the Gospel, especially through the non-profit my wife and I formed." The Sappingtons have also elected to invest in their children by homeschooling them, further increasing their flexibility for ministry.

As a business owner, Steve has also learned how to take advantage of more tax saving opportunities. Unlike his time at the brokerage firm, he is now able to customize the selection of products and equipment that he uses to serve his clients. This makes his services both unique and particularly suited to his clients' needs.

All three BE courses helped Steve find new ways to make his business a ministry. "I am so thankful for how God has used Patrice to illuminate what God's Word says about business. I had devoted years to studying how to work 'as unto the Lord and not men,' but Patrice's teachings made all of my foundational work look like baby steps," Steve shares. "Ultimately, we have been privileged to be used by God to bless others, in large part because we operate a business that strives to glorify God daily."

CHAPTER FIFTEEN
DR. RASHIDA COHEN
_ADVANTAGE REHABILITATION & WELLNESS CENTER

"I loved having a big family!" Dr. Rashida Cohen laughs as she recalls what it was like to have six younger brothers and sisters. Growing up all over Africa—The Ivory Coast, Niger, and Egypt—Rashida and her siblings were never bored. They always had enough players for cricket, soccer, or any other game even when their neighborhood friends had to go home.

God gave Rashida a heart to care for others from a young age. "My parents never pushed me to take care of my siblings, but as the oldest child I automatically took on responsibility." That sense of responsibility also earned her an academic record that landed her a spot at Spelman College in Atlanta while the rest of her family settled in Washington, DC. By her senior year, a family friend named Dr. Henderson was encouraging her to apply to chiropractic school.

"I had never considered chiropractic school since I didn't even know what a chiropractor was!" Dr. Cohen explains. As she pondered this strange advice, she happened to meet a chiropractor at the gym when she was working out. They struck up a conversation and she asked him if she could visit his office to learn more about the field.

"It was definitely the Lord," she declares. "Not only did I apply to chiropractic school, I was accepted and received a full scholarship. Once I started the program, I knew this was a profession that I could love

89

forever." Rashida spent time with Dr. Henderson on her visits home and when she graduated from chiropractic school, Dr. Henderson had a job for her in Washington, D.C.

Dr. Cohen had received excellent training in her profession and felt very confident to begin work as a chiropractor. However, she would soon realize that there was one crucial aspect of being a doctor that her graduate studies had neglected.

"When I graduated from chiropractic school, I had only had eleven weeks of business training. Like most doctors, I had no idea what a profit and loss statement was. I had no idea how to run the business side of a practice," Dr. Cohen explains. No course in her many years of schooling had taught her how to deal with clients who did not pay or how to calculate the number of patients the practice needed to cover its overhead costs. Yet these were the realities she faced when she went to work for Dr. Henderson.

The burden of running a business without adequate training was taking its toll on Dr. Henderson too; she was so burned out, in fact, that she decided to sell her practice. Rashida continued to work for Dr. Henderson and even considered purchasing the practice from her, but felt that she needed more entrepreneurial training first.

"By the time I got to BE, I was pretty stressed out. Life in DC was very expensive, and my patient load felt overwhelming. BE reminded me that the business belonged to God, not to me, and that my situation was not too big for Jesus to handle. The first part of BE was so encouraging that I actually took it twice."

Ultimately, the encouragement Rashida received from BE was translated into a much healthier business. Dr. Cohen's jar of oil, her doctorate in chiropractic, was now augmented by a sound business plan. She was able to implement that plan by using her own money and credit cards to finance her practice. Now Dr. Cohen and her husband Marlon are the founders and stewards of Advantage Rehabilitation and Wellness Center located in downtown Washington, DC.

Dr. Cohen received an exhortation to enlist the help of others, including her family, and today her business blesses those same people. Just as the widow's sons were blessed when they helped her pour the oil into jars, Advantage Rehabilitation and Wellness Center now employs five additional staff including Dr. Cohen's mother and some of her sisters.

"My family cares a great deal about our business. It is wonderful to know that I have employees who will neither take advantage of me nor work against our mission. I am so glad to be able to provide them with an income by which they can support themselves and our family," Dr. Cohen shares.

Although Dr. Cohen had to finance the start of her practice, her determination to borrow to produce and not to consume has allowed her to pay off her debts and live on the rest. Advantage Rehabilitation and Wellness Center's annual revenue has grown to nearly a million dollars with healthy profit margins in a competitive industry. Its growing clientele has enabled the Cohens to seek out a larger facility and make plans to acquire two new centers in the near future.

Dr. Cohen enthusiastically shares with everyone the fact that Biblical Entrepreneurship laid the foundation that launched her into business successfully. Her graduate school made her a doctor, but BE turned her into a Kingdom-minded businesswoman. Dr. Cohen is an active member of her local church and a regular financial supporter of Nehemiah Project International Ministries. She also travels throughout the country to encourage other young doctors to open their own businesses the right way.

"I am the membership chair for the American Black Chiropractic Association. Every year, I travel to schools and speak to students at different undergraduate institutions about becoming a chiropractor. As a result, I am happy to receive interested students in our office throughout the year and am thrilled when many of them decide to go into the chiropractic field." Dr. Cohen has also encouraged many colleagues in the medical profession who have spent time at her facility to discover what makes her practice so unique and successful.

The biblical foundation for Dr. Cohen's business is apparent in the way she runs her center as well as the way she serves her patients. "When my patients allow me to, I am able to pray with them either before or after treatment. It is wonderful to see those prayers answered," she explains. She also spends time privately praying for all of her patients, asking God to specifically guide her hands as she works with each one of them. Sometimes God even opens the door for ministry beyond her office walls.

"One of my patients who was far from her own family came to my parents' home last Christmas and really felt like a member of our family during her time in Washington, D.C.," Dr. Cohen recalls. "She had no friends here and told me that she picked my office out of many. I truly believe that God led her here so we could support her during her trying time away." The two continued to pray together during just about every visit, and remained a blessing in each other's lives throughout the patient's time in the area.

Like all doctors, Rashida knows her call is to heal. "I have literally seen miracles happen," she reflects. "Patients have come to us who could not use their hands or their legs, and are headed for surgery. I have seen them return to normal limb function without the risks and potential complications of surgery. I have seen babies in a breech position just before their due date turn to a head down position so their mothers could give birth naturally. Jesus is powerful!!!"

Thanks to following the teachings of Scripture, Dr. Cohen is able to bring excellent care through an excellent business model. Her practice not only blesses her financially, but is also a blessing to her family, her patients and to the community it serves.

CHAPTER SIXTEEN
GLENN REPPLE
— G.A. REPPLE & COMPANY

GLENN came from a long line of entrepreneurs going all the way back to a grandfather who owned his own business. He had always been a savvy investor, dealing in real estate and other commodities. However, in 1982 he decided to take the treasure of his knowledge and experience to market by becoming a registered Broker Dealer and Investment Advisor.

Glenn, like the widow, had to mix his assets with borrowed assets in order to share his expertise with others. "I borrowed money on a line of credit to finance the furniture and equipment to start the business," he explains.

"God will use whatever it takes to get your attention. He used the desert for the Israelites. For me it was business collapse. I thought we had it made. We had just won the Chamber of Commerce small business award for growth. We were being quoted regularly on TV, radio, and in the newspapers. Our company had grown from just a dream to a revenue producing machine. We looked good on the outside. Our office space was the best.

"Yet we were 3 months behind in our rent. We had negotiated a five year lease with the first year with no payments. The rent was $14,000 per month. So I figured we saved $168,000 of money by not having to pay rent for a year. Because we were behind in the rent the lease was being called and the landlord wanted us to move. The amount of rent due now was over $300,000. They wanted it now.

"At the same time we had lines of credit at the maximum. The bank that we did business with was being sold and the new bank wanted the line of credit paid in full. Even though we were current and paid on time, they wanted their money now.

"In addition to this, the tax reform act of 1986 had been signed that impacted real estate and the savings and loan business. We were heavily invested in real estate and very leveraged. This law closed down the deductions for many tax favored investments and tax shelters such as real estate. Our revenue was being threatened. We knew that we could not maintain the same level of income. We were already behind in our rent with the landlord calling our lease and the bank calling our line of credit.

"We had unhappy investors. Many real estate companies were filing for bankruptcy. Investors were suffering from potential loss.

"We were in a squeeze. There seemed to be no way out. This was all happening in the fourth quarter of 1987. I began seeking God's guidance and direction. I sensed that the Lord was hitting me over the head with a two by four telling me that I had violated many of HIS laws. My wife had disagreed with the borrowing. Because the Lord was convicting me to be debt free, I felt that we needed to teach this to our advisors and clients. In October of 1987 I prayed, 'Lord remove those people in our company that you want removed and bring in those that you want. I commit to never ever borrow money again.' I sensed the Lord speaking to me saying, 'Stop your advertising and marketing, trust Me I am the best marketer, I will send you all the people you need.'

"I began to step out in obedience to what I sensed the Lord was telling me. The Financial Advisors did not take well to the idea that we were going to stop all advertising and marketing. They had become dependent on marketing. This meant that they would have to go out and fish rather than be given the fish, which had been a treat to them.

"The advisors did not take well to my announcement that we should help people pay off their mortgage and other debt obligations. This meant that money that could have been used for investment would be used to reduce debt. This meant that they would lose revenue.

"We had a small mortgage company. We closed the company out of conviction that we wanted to get people out of debt rather than encourage debt.

"Then the bomb happened that seemed to be the devastating final blow. All of the Financial Advisors resigned at once. They left and set up a competing business. Those Financial Advisors could not see how G. A. Repple and Company would survive. This meant that our revenue would be cut severely. We needed this revenue to support the debt service.

"I bottomed. My pride and ego was broken. I began to trust God for guidance. My way was not working. My family had suffered because of my desire to get rich. My selfish desires needed to be changed and focused on God. My desire to have a big company, be important, be recognized, and enjoy the pleasures of life, now did not seem as important as trusting the God of my salvation and redemption. It is much easier to see God in brokenness. My brokenness was the beginning to the restoration and transformation of myself, our family, and our company.

"Our revenue went down by 70% in 1988, the next year. We began to sell off assets and maintained just enough to have our daily bread each day. We became content to live one day at a time. Because the advisors had left, our expenses also went down proportionally and we began to make a profit. We negotiated with the landlord and the bank. Although we did not see it at the time, it is obvious that God's hand of mercy was on us. God had orchestrated all of this for my good. What had been perceived as bad turned out to be the molding and shaping that I needed in my life and also in the company. We began to build on a solid ground. Over a period of about seven years the business became debt free and as a family we paid off all mortgages and debts. We had become free from debt.

"Over the next years advisors began to join us again. As our vision moved toward becoming a Kingdom business and workplace ministry, God brought us the people who would help fulfill His mission. Our response to God brought us an increase of almost a hundred fold. God blessed us and our family. We have been able to attract some great people who desire to serve others. We have seen God transform my life, our family, and the business. Praise be to God.

"What seemed to be a bad experience with a lot of suffering turned out to be for the good of all. God used the circumstances to teach me contentment in all things. He taught me to trust Him in all circumstances. He taught me that He is in control and will work everything out for my best. He taught me that He does have rules that He wants me to follow.

"When I break His rules, there are consequences. He taught me about debt; it is better to be a lender than a debtor because the debtor is a slave to the lender.

"In the process, many of the people around us helped the venture to prosper. My wife invested the most, especially at first. My son, Bryan, was helpful as well. I also sought the expertise of many coaches and advisors along the way, noting that the most helpful advice came from a biblical perspective."

G. A. Repple and Company now has 80 Branch Offices and is licensed in all 50 States. They have 15,000 customers and have been in business for over 25 years. They are financial planners who help people structure their affairs to be financially free. They also provide tax planning, estate planning, charitable planning, and risk management services.

A mutual friend introduced Glenn to Patrice. Patrice was able to give Glenn long distance training in BE concepts. After learning the principles and meeting with the directors of the Nehemiah Project, Glenn sensed that God wanted him to come on board. "I was convicted that BE was something that I could take to the Financial Planning marketplace," he explains.

His business has become a tremendous success, allowing his family to pay off all its debts and employ many other people. They have been able to provide great benefits to their employees and also give back to the community.

CHAPTER SEVENTEEN

FRANK REYNOLDS

FRANK REYNOLDS WEALTH MANAGEMENT

"LOTS of folks would say that I graduated from the school of hard knocks," Frank laughs. "I didn't get a lot of college experience because I had to work. However, I developed a very practical skill set: communication, organization, planning, analysis, and management." Frank was actually a manager for ten years before taking the treasure of his hard-earned skill set to market in 1986.

Frank did not require a large amount of start-up capital to launch his business, so he did not need to borrow money initially. From the very beginning, Frank was not chasing money; he was pursuing the vision of God. "I did not have significant financial resources when I established my new practice, but I had a thirst for learning and a faith in God that sustained me in the early years," he explains. Instead of going for the wealthiest clients he could find, Frank wanted to serve and edify the body of Christ. His business provides financial management services specifically designed for Christian families and Christian ministries.

"We help Christian families with four distinct services: Christian financial planning and estate design, investment portfolio strategies, insurance counseling, and planned giving," Frank explains. "Depending upon their needs, clients may utilize one or more of our services. Additionally, we serve Christian ministries by helping them develop and implement strategic and operational plans for their financial support. We also offer stewardship training and donor development resources, benefit programs for ministry staff, financing resources for ministry expansion, as well as donor development processes to help maximize income gifts, asset gifts, planned gifts, and estate gifts."

Like many entrepreneurs, Frank found day-to-day operations and administration to be one of the largest potential distractions from the eternal purpose for which God has given him the business. "As a Christian financial planner, I had to decide whether I would use the same processes as my secular counterparts, or take a stand by using biblical processes," Frank explains. "My most potent weapons in overcoming these distractions and relying on biblical practices are prayer, Bible study, practicing stewardship of all that God has given me, and developing mentoring relationships with other Christian professionals."

Overall this required Frank to focus on helping his clients to understand the purpose of maximizing their temporary net worth while simultaneously maximizing their return on that worth. He has also developed mentoring relationships both inside and outside his industry. He has even benefited from the wisdom of non-Christians who are committed to ethical standards and who understand what it takes to run a successful business.

In addition to Christian financial professionals like Glenn Repple of G.A. Repple & Company, Ron Blue of Kingdom Advisors, and ministry leaders like Ray Lyne of Lifestyle Giving, Frank cites his wife as a key figure in his business. "My wife, Maret, is also my business partner and has been a vital part in helping me to implement God's vision for this business," he explains. Yet his most important advisor is the Lord Himself. "My top priority is seeking counsel from the Lord God Almighty on a consistent basis."

Frank had been a Biblical Entrepreneur for a dozen years before he ever connected with Patrice and took a BE class. However, he found the experience very edifying. "BE did a wonderful job of affirming how marketplace ministry should operate," Frank says. "It also enhanced my ability to communicate our vision to clients, advisors, and ministry leaders. I have been pleased to offer it as a resource to help friends and clients learn how to function successfully in marketplace ministry, and my wife found it very beneficial as well."

Frank Reynolds Wealth Management currently serves 250 individuals and 12 ministries, yet there have been many times when Frank had to believe God for miraculous intervention. "It has been my experience in all areas of my life that the Lord God Almighty likes to show up at the last minute," Frank recalls. "While we have been extremely blessed over the years, there have been a number of times where finances became difficult, staffing became challenging, or relationships with vendors and clients became strained. In every one of those situations, I have seen God deliver in miraculous and incredible ways. God has never left me or forsaken me, even though there have been times when I struggled with doubt. I have found that if I wait on the Lord, He always delivers in the best way possible."

As Frank and his wife have waited on God, He has blessed them with financial freedom and much more. "The business God has given me to manage has improved my personal financial situation in ways that I could never have imagined," Frank explains. "We are able to do things now that I never would have believed possible in my twenties. Yet even more precious than the financial blessings are the friendships and other relationships that God has given us as well as the strengthening of our individual relationships with God. I encourage all Christians to consider what marketplace ministry can do for them, their family, and their walk with God."

NOTHING BUT A JAR OF OIL

CHAPTER EIGHTEEN
TYRONE GRIGSBY
NETWORK SOLUTIONS

EVERYONE dreams of getting in on the ground floor of something big: buying shares of Microsoft before personal computers became ubiquitous or landing the contract to build all the cell phone towers in Southeast Asia. Tyrone Grigsby, a Biblical Entrepreneur, lived that dream. He started Network Solutions in 1979 which later became the first Internet registration company in the world.

One of Tyrone's greatest treasures was his education, in which he had invested a great deal. "I obtained business management training at Howard University, The University of Connecticut, and American Management Association with an emphasis on corporate finance and planning," Tyrone explains. Nevertheless his understanding of the business world went beyond just the classroom. "I also gained practical experience as a financial analyst in the corporate finance department of a major insurance company, as a minority shareholder in a computer services company, as a real estate developer, and in various other small business endeavors."

In the late 1970s, foreseeing the incredible impact that computers would have on the business world, Tyrone started Network Solutions with three other partners. Like the widow, he did not possess sufficient resources to carry his oil to market, so he took out loans and a second mortgage on his house. However he actually needed the startup capital before any bank would consider loaning him money for his venture. At that point, he had to enlist the help of those around him, including a good friend, John Booker, who was a fellow small business owner.

"John is a true friend and made numerous unsecured 'handshake' loans during the early years, before major bank financing was available to us," Tyrone recalls.

Many people who look at Tyrone now would assume that he has benefited from good luck all of his life; however, he faced many obstacles before he obtained his financial victory. Instead of allowing those obstacles to distract him, he simply tackled them one at a time.

"We faced the typical biases against small businesses and minority-owned businesses," Tyrone explains. Before Network Solutions was well established, it was difficult to convince big clients that they could do the job. "We also had difficulty recruiting competent, honest, reliable employees, and of course we were undercapitalized."

God, in His sovereignty, offered a variety of solutions to the problems they faced. "We gained entry into the federal government's small/minority set-aside programs which enabled us to obtain a foothold with government contracts," Tyrone explains. "We then provided extraordinarily high-quality, high-demand services and products to our clients who in turn provided us with excellent references to other clients and banks." Once it began to establish a track record, Network Solutions was ready to grow. Once again, the company had to mix borrowed assets with what it had in order to take the business to the next level, and ultimately set itself up for a big break.

"Our strong referrals enabled us to obtain the bank financing to accelerate our marketing and fuel the rapid growth of our company during the 1980s and early 1990s. This also put us in position to be selected by the Bureau of Standards to develop the Internet registration process," he shares. They made other strategic moves as well. "We hired non-minority employees and advisors who ran interference for us so that the race of our ownership wouldn't hinder our growth. This helped us break into networks of people and opportunities that ultimately made our ride to the top a lot smoother."

Tyrone's initial struggle to find qualified personnel with strong character ended up being a blessing for others. "We provided opportunities for minorities and college graduates who had no work experience, but demonstrated excellent work ethics. We knew we could build our company with those kinds of people."

In addition to prayerful strategic planning, Tyrone is deeply grateful for the people around him whose help he was able to enlist from the beginning. Besides his friend John, bankers Paul Brammel, Joe Pipitone and Harry Fisher made loans to the company at crucial junctures in its growth, including a time it was on the brink of bankruptcy. Arthur Scandrett, the small business liaison officer at the Department of Labor, facilitated the award of a systems development and network management contract there that grew from a $100,000 project to $10,000,000.

"There are really too many people to mention," Tyrone says of those who helped make Network Solutions a success. "Attorney John Woods introduced me to key people who enabled us to fight through or avoid various bureaucratic barriers. Paul Brown, an Associate Director with the U.S. Small Business Administration, approved our application for inclusion in the federal government's minority set-aside program after others in the agency had denied us." All of these people were pivotal in making Network Solutions and its owners financially victorious.

Although BE did not exist when Tyrone was building Network Solutions, at his initial connection with the ministry he found it to be an extension of what the Lord had already been showing him. "From the beginning, I studied the teachings of [Christian finance author] Larry Burkett, my pastor, and of course I spent personal time in the Bible. I continually adjusted my management practices to align with biblical principles. The BE program further validated and expanded the teachings I had received. Most importantly, the BE training revealed to me that my business is a tool God gave me to accomplish His purpose for my life. I have always held Deuteronomy 8:18 close to my heart: 'And you shall remember the Lord your God, for it is He who gives you power to get wealth, that He may establish His covenant which He swore to your fathers, as it is this day.'"

Ultimately, Tyrone was able to sell Network Solutions in 1995 and retire. He has used his financial freedom to sow into the Kingdom of God and fund the Great Commission. "I have come to realize that my efforts alone did not enable me to accomplish anything, but instead it was the grace and favor of God. How else could I have escaped bankruptcy to get in on the ground floor in a new industry that has radically changed how the world communicates? This business has enabled me to support God's work and allowed me to be a role model to other Christians and entrepreneurs."

Chapter Nineteen

Linda Sattgast

Scrapper's Guide

LINDA Sattgast was born to scrapbook. "At the age of six, I started writing letters to my parents every week," Linda recalls. "They were on the mission field in El Salvador, and I was in boarding school like many missionary kids of that era. I would recount my activities of the week in my letters, and the older I grew, the more detailed they became. When I was ten, I received a one-year diary for Christmas. I wrote in my journal nearly every day from that time until my senior year of high school."

Linda's habit of recording important events and thoughts made scrapbooking a natural fit for her. "I was introduced to paper and scissors scrapbooking in 1996 and immediately fell in love with the concept of combining family photos with journaling and art. Our entire family still cherishes the three full albums I created recording our road trip around the entire United States."

Linda finished college as a trained x-ray technician and married Charlie, a man from an entrepreneurial family that owned two stores. Accustomed to the life of the small business owner, Charlie tried a couple of ventures with his new bride that were profitable, but did not quite pay all the bills. As long as Linda continued working at the hospital, however, they had more than enough.

The Sattgasts learned an early lesson about the dangers of borrowing to consume instead of to produce. They bought a new car after the birth of their first child and found themselves struggling to make payments while Linda stayed home with their new baby. "Given our financial situation at the time, we should not have bought a brand new car. We could have purchased a good, used car for a price within our means," she explains.

Linda's first solo business venture was only tangentially related to scrapbooking: she became a successful children's author, publishing several books that collectively sold over one million copies. The couple quickly followed Elisha's admonition to the widow and used their profits to pay off their debt. "I'll never forget the arrival of a substantial royalty check that enabled us to pay off the car in full. Oh, happy day!"

Even without the car payment, however, the Sattgasts were still far from financial freedom. With the arrival of their son and later their daughter, Linda longed to be home with the children, but without her salary from the hospital, they were forced to sell their possessions to buy groceries. They settled on a stressful in-between arrangement: juggling schedules to make sure their children did not have to go to daycare, but sacrificing sleep and time together as a family.

As they continued to work hard and do all that they knew to do, the Lord intervened supernaturally. In what little spare time she had, Linda began using her new digital camera and color printer to continue her scrapbooking hobby. One night, the Lord inspired her with a brand new concept. "I awoke at 3:00 a.m. with a fully formed idea: I could create 12" x 12" scrapbook pages (the popular scrapbooking size) on the computer. I could print the entire page on my new, large format printer. Immediately I knew that this idea would be big. I would be able to teach this technique to others and make millions of dollars because I knew everyone would be as thrilled about the concept of computer scrapbooking as I was!"

Linda had realized that by utilizing particular software programs, entire pages could be laid out on the computer with limitless design possibilities. No more scissors and glue! "I was so excited I couldn't sleep. Immediately I began to sketch out ideas for my first digital scrapbook pages—never mind that I knew nothing about computers or photo editing programs!" With the support of her husband, Linda set to work learning Photoshop and related software programs. In a few weeks, she began to create and print her digital scrapbook pages, just as she envisioned.

Linda had learned the skills, and now the question was how to bring this new treasure to market. She and Charlie determined that an instructional video would work best. For the next eighteen months they used their extra time and Linda's book royalties to produce this new DVD. They could not afford to hire professionals, so they learned to create and edit videos and Charlie learned to build a website to promote their new product.

Without a large publicity budget, Linda and Charlie enlisted the help of loved ones to launch their new business. "The week I turned fifty we officially started ScrappersGuide.com by sending out our first online newsletter to everyone in our family and any friends we could think of, inviting them to sign up for a free subscription," Linda explains. They also attended scrapbooking trade shows to demonstrate their new technique, gaining numerous customers that way as well.

"Probably my biggest distraction was working another job while trying to start and run Scrapper's Guide," Linda recalls. "We needed to do it that way to stay out of debt, but it was hard to divide my attention between two demanding careers." In the end, however, it was Linda's determination that ruled the day. "By God's grace I simply did what I could in the time that I had and refused to give up."

It turned out that the Lord inspired Linda just in time for the digital revolution. Scrapper's Guide now provides computer training and scrapbooking supplies to over 22,000 digital scrapbookers; helping them create scrapbook pages using Photoshop or Photoshop Elements.

Linda explains how digital scrapbooking has changed the entire industry. "Forums and galleries are the online equivalent of traditional "crop" gatherings for scissor and glue scrapbooking. We have a forum and gallery for our members and occasionally sponsor contests and challenges to encourage participation and excellence."

Linda continued to work full time at the hospital and run Scrapper's Guide along with Charlie for the first three years of the business. The business grew and their financial situation improved.

Then Linda had a heart attack. "I knew I was working too hard," Linda admits. "I asked God what I should do. He gave me the idea of starting a premier membership program that would enable me to work half time." She and Charlie immediately created Digital Scrapper Premier, a program for digital scrapbookers who wanted to receive ongoing training videos and scrapbooking supplies at a discount. Linda cut back her hours at the hospital and seemed to be doing better.

"A year later the membership program was going well, but I was still working too much, and I had another minor heart attack," Linda explains. Linda's health challenges became both a worry and a distraction as she and Charlie tried to build the business and keep their household running. Again, they sought God for guidance. They decided that it was time to take a step of faith and give up Linda's steady income from the hospital.

Linda and Charlie attended BE when they wanted to take Scrapper's Guide beyond the status of a "mom and pop" business. They came for business expertise but received so much more. "What I didn't expect when I took the class was the radical change in perspective it would give me," Linda explains. "I was a Christian and I had a business, but I realized during BE that it wasn't really a Kingdom business. I came home after the first class overwhelmed with a fresh understanding of biblical passages I had read over and over but had never applied to business."

This major shift in perspective allowed Linda to see Scrapper's Guide as God's business. God, in turn, has continually proven Himself faithful by opening doors for her professionally. Adobe, the well-known software company that makes the programs Linda uses in her digital scrapbooking, responded positively to her initial inquiry when she launched her business. "Before we launched Scrapper's Guide I contacted Adobe to make sure we were within their guidelines for using their software in our video," she explains. "They invited me to join the Beta team that tests the new program upgrades. Since that time I've taught for Adobe at various trade shows and webinars, and they partnered with me at a number of scrapbooking trade shows to promote my training." They have even given Linda the title of "Adobe's Scrapbooking Expert"!

God rewarded Charlie and Linda's step of faith by further prospering their business and preserving Linda's health. "Besides allowing me to quit my job as an X-ray tech, Scrapper's Guide paid for college for both our children and allowed Charlie to complete his master's degree in Pastoral Studies as he'd always dreamed," Linda recounts gratefully. "Recently Adobe purchased a large number of my training CDs to put in the box with their Photoshop Elements software program for distribution to Costco stores.

"We're now asking God to bless Scrapper's Guide enough so Charlie can devote himself full-time to ministry," she continues. "We believe that in addition to allowing us to retire from active business, we will be able to financially support the work of God's Kingdom even beyond our tithe."

PART THREE

WORKBOOK

7 STEPS
TO
ACHIEVING
YOUR OWN
FINANCIAL
VICTORY

NOTHING BUT A JAR OF OIL

Chapter Twenty
Workbook

1. **Assess Your Assets—What are your current assets?**

   ◆ TREASURES—money you possess in cash

   _____

   _____

   ◆ INVESTMENTS—money you have invested in the stock market or in other businesses that you can turn into cash

   _____

   _____

   ◆ IDEAS—unique concepts that you can turn into a product or service that can generate income

   _____

   _____

   ◆ ABILITIES—skills that you can use to generate revenue

   _____

   _____

   ◆ POSSESSIONS—such as houses, cars, jewelry, clothes, shoes, furniture, equipment, land, etc.

   _____

   _____

◆ RELATIONSHIPS—people you know who can help you achieve your goals

_____

_____

◆ SPIRITUAL GIFTS—Holy-Spirit-led gifts such as service, giving, mercy, that enhance your business

_____

_____

◆ EXPERIENCES—things you have done before such as a job, a business, or a project

_____

_____

◆ Do you recognize that God has given you talents in line with your abilities and He expects you to use them profitably?

☐ Yes   ☐ No

◆ Are you committed to using your talents to generate revenue and become financially free so that you can become a lender and not a borrower?

☐ Yes   ☐ No

◆ How can you turn these assets you have just listed into a business that can allow you to generate income to become financially free? What type of business can you start?

_____

_____

2. Borrow to Produce—Do you need equity and debt financing in order to produce?

⬥ How much consumer debt do you currently have? What is the source? What was its purpose? What is your projected timeline for paying it off?

_____

_____

_____

⬥ If you do not have enough assets to generate revenue, how much will you need from other sources?

_____

_____

⬥ Will you use debt or equity financing? Why?

_____

_____

_____

⬥ When do you plan to repay the loan [or what is the Return on Investment (ROI) for the investors]?

_____

_____

⬥ Are you committed to debt-free living, saying no to consumer debt and putting your complete trust in God's ability to provide for your needs? Are you committed to short-term borrowing (only to produce) when necessary, with a commitment to repay back the loan as soon as possible? ☐ Yes ☐ No

Why

_____

_____

3. Block Out All Distractions—list the various activities, people, and things that have kept you distracted from achieving your goals.

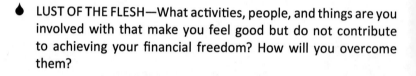 LUST OF THE EYE—What activities, people, and things attract your eyes but do not contribute to achieving your financial freedom? How will you overcome them?

_____

_____

_____

◆ LUST OF THE FLESH—What activities, people, and things are you involved with that make you feel good but do not contribute to achieving your financial freedom? How will you overcome them?

_____

_____

_____

◆ PRIDE OF LIFE—What activities, people, and things are you involved with that make you feel important but do not contribute to achieving your financial freedom? How will you overcome them?

_____

_____

_____

◆ Are you committed to blocking out all distractions by rejecting the activities, people, or things that feed the lust of your eyes, the lust of your flesh, and build your pride without contributing to your financial freedom?

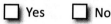 ☐ Yes   ☐ No

4. Enlist the Help of Others

- Are you ready for help? If not, when do you think you will need help?

_____

_____

_____

- What type of help do you need? List and describe the areas where you need help.

_____

_____

_____

_____

- What type of person(s) are you looking for? Describe the gifts, skills, personalities, and experiences of the people you need.

_____

_____

_____

_____

- What's in it for them? List the various benefits for those helping you realize your goals.

_____

_____

_____

_____

Start with those closest to you—consider your children, brothers, sisters, cousins, nieces, nephews, friends, co-workers, etc. Who among them can help you?

_____

_____

_____

_____

 Do not limit yourself to those you know—if you cannot find help amont those you know, look beyond your acquaintences. What organizations, conferences, and events can you attend where you can meet the type of people you are looking for? Who can refer you to someone you need but do not know?

_____

_____

_____

_____

 SHOW APPRECIATION—How will you demonstrate appreciation to those who will help you?

_____

_____

_____

_____

5. Trust God for the Supernatural

🔹 Have you done all that you need to do? Make a list of the things that will improve your situation that are still in your control to accomplish.

_____

_____

_____

_____

🔹 Are you living a holy life? Make a list of the known sins in your life that you must overcome and explain how you will overcome them.

_____

_____

_____

_____

🔹 Do you tithe? (A tithe is the first 10% of gross personal income. You must tithe to your local church from your personal income. If you have a business, you should tithe on the net income from your business.)

☐ Yes   ☐ No

🔹 Do you give generously? (You cannot give an offering unless you first tithe.)

☐ Yes   ☐ No

NOTE: Give offerings, alms, and however the Lord leads you. Remember you are not giving so you can receive, but rather as an act of obedience and appreciation to God.

◆ If you do not tithe and give consistently, how will you address this?

_____

_____

_____

_____

◆ Do you pray and fast regularly?

☐ Yes   ☐ No

◆ Make a list of your concerns that require God to move supernaturally. Commit to praying and fasting.

_____

_____

_____

_____

_____

_____

_____

_____

6. Sell (Your Product or Service) for Profit

♦ List and describe the products and services that you want to sell, including features and benefits.

_____

_____

_____

_____

_____

_____

♦ Do you believe these products and services can provide value to others?　　☐ Yes　　☐ No

♦ What needs can they meet in the lives of others?

_____

_____

_____

_____

♦ Who are your customers? Profile your top three customers. Include their age, race, religious affiliation, income, geographic location, tastes, preferences, and special needs. How many of these people exist? Are there enough of them to support your business?

_____

_____

_____

_____

_____
_____
_____
_____

♦ How do you know when your customer is ready to buy? How will you track them as they become ready?

_____
_____
_____
_____

♦ How will you close the sale? Write out your sales process in detail beginning with how you will make the appeal, and ending with how you will close the deal.

_____
_____
_____
_____
_____

♦ Explain which types of payments you will receive and why?

_____
_____
_____
_____

● How will you show appreciation to your customers?

_____

_____

_____

_____

Pricing Your Product or Service

● What are your costs?

_____

_____

_____

_____

● What are your competitors charging? Indentify three of your competitors and list their products, services, and prices.

1. _____

_____

2. _____

_____

3. _____

_____

What are your customers willing to spend? Conduct a survey or focus group with various prices and determine what your customers are willing to pay.

_____

_____

_____

_____

_____

 What are the intangible benefits of your product or service? List the features of your product or service and explain the needs it meets in the lives of your customers. Does it save them money or make them money? How does it enhance their lives or protect them?

_____

_____

_____

_____

_____

What will be your mark-up percentage? Base this on your cost, what your customers are willing to pay, what your competitors are charging, and what is the intangible value of your product or service. Explain.

_____

_____

_____

_____

_____

7. Pay Your Debts and Live on the Rest

- Use the budget sheet found on www.NothingButAJarOfOil.com. Develop a personal budget for your household, making sure to Include every conceivable expense. Keep in mind the ratios we discussed in the last chapter.

- Based on your debt situation, develop a debt-free plan using the guideline of setting aside at least 20% of your income towards debt payment. Develop a schedule for your debt payments. (Do this on your own paper.)

- Using your debt-free plan, how long will it take you to become debt free?

  _____

  _____

- Make a list of the major expenses you anticipate using your savings to purchase once you are debt free.

  _____

  _____

  _____

  _____

  _____

  _____

  _____

  _____

  _____

♦ Make a savings plan to commit 10% of your income for "rainy days". (Work this out on your own paper.)

♦ Talk with a financial planner to determine the type of investments that may be available for your extra money so that you can make your money start working for you. Make sure your financial planner shares your moral values and will not place your funds in any industries that God would not bless.

MEET THE AUTHORS

PATRICE TSAGUE

A dynamic teacher of God's Word, Patrice Tsague is anointed with a unique ability to blend entrepreneurship principles with biblical truths. Patrice is the author of several books including the *Biblical Entrepreneurship Coaching Guide, Biblical Principles of Starting and Operating a Business,* and *Nothing but a Jar of Oil.* Along with his wife, Gina, he created the Biblical Entrepreneurship Certificate Training Program to teach business owners how to fulfill God's plan for their lives through their business. He is a Biblical Entrepreneurship Certified Instructor with over ten years of experience as a business teacher. He is also a coach/consultant for a number of start-up, small, and medium-sized companies and creator of *Biblical Principles for Starting and Operating a Business: The Biblical Entrepreneurship Marketplace Series.* Patrice serves as Chief Servant Officer of Nehemiah Project International Ministries and of P.G. and Associates. He is chaplain for the National Association of Christian Financial Advisors (NACFC) and publishes a weekly e-devotional. Patrice Tsague is a licensed minister with Bethel World Outreach Ministries and serves as Executive Director of Bethel World Ministries International. He and his wife have two children, Gabrielle and Danielle.

CONTACT
Nehemiah Project International Ministries
242188 Arena Stage Ct. | Damascus, MD 20872
877-916-1180 | www.nehemiahproject.org

MELVIN B. MOORING

For the past 9 years, Melving B. Mooring has served as the Chief Financial Officer of a privately owned company with revenues over $26 million. This company provides promotional gift items to unions, and private and government entities across the Washington Metropolitan Area. Mr. Mooring used his 27 years in accounting to begin Mooring &Associates, where he serves as President and Chief Financial Officer. Mooring & Associates is a corporation that handles individual and corporate tax returns, corporate start-up support, financial planning, and short and long term investment strategies. Mr. Mooring is widely experienced in non-profit, government, and corporate accounting. One of his cherished accomplishments was negotiating lower rates from Child Welfare contractors to enable children to have additional funding for education, clothing, and recreational activities. Mr. Mooring is happily married to Beverley Boothe-Mooring for six years, and he is the father of Melvin Mooring II.

CONTACT
Mooring & Associates
7320 Heritage Village Plaza | Ste. 202 | Gainesville, VA 20155
703-754-0989 | www.mooringandassociates.com
Workshops & Financial Planning

Resources

NPIM Overview

The Nehemiah Project International Ministries, Inc. (NPIM) is a nonprofit, tax exempt, business training, and business support service organization that provides high quality, comprehensive, transformational, biblically-based entrepreneurship curricula and resources.

Most graduates of the program operate small to medium-sized kingdom companies. The course is offered online and live. It is currently available in the United States, Mexico, Ukraine, Europe, and Cameroon (Central Africa). The course is endorsed by Regent Center for Entrepreneurship, the National Association of Christian Financial Counselors, the Timothy Plan, and G.A. Repple and Company.

Mission

To equip and empower individuals to steward God's resources through biblically-based, entrepreneurial training, thereby helping them fulfill God's plan for their lives.

Motto

Helping people fulfill God's plan for their lives through business.

Vision

To transform the marketplace with the gospel of the Lord Jesus Christ, one entrepreneur at a time, with the ultimate goal to create a community of Kingdom business stewards who provide God-honoring services and products in a God-honoring way, and are contributing to the fulfillment of the Great Commission.

Comparative Advantage

We provide high-quality, comprehensive, transformational, biblically-based entrepreneurship curricula and resources.

Products and Services

Biblical Entrepreneurship (BE) is a proprietary, comprehensive, transformational business discipleship course, created and distributed by Nehemiah Project International Ministries. The program provides a strong mix of core business concepts and biblical principles. Some of the courses offered include **Principles of Biblical Entrepreneurship (BE I), Practices of Biblical Entrepreneurship (BE II),** and **Planning a Kingdom Business (BE III).**

The cost of the BE program (BE I, BE II, and BE III) including materials, is currently $1795.00. The cost for Teacher Certification Training is $1200 per person.

Students who complete the entire course (BE I, BE II, and BE III) participate in a business plan competition and receive a Biblical Entrepreneurship Certificate through NPIM and Regent Center for Entrepreneurship.

Other training programs in development include:

- The Biblical Executive Business Management Certificate Program
- The Kingdom Executive Business Management Certificate Program
- Doing Business with Purpose and Profitability Certificate Program
- Biblical Entrepreneurship Certificate Program for Youth

To register for an upcoming class visit our website at **www.nehemiahproject.org** or call us at **1-877-916-1180** or contact the BE Distributor nearest you.

OTHER BOOKS BY PATRICE TSAGUE

BIBLICAL PRINCIPLES FOR STARTING & OPERATING A BUSINESS: The Biblical Entrepreneurship Marketplace Series

—————————————————————— Paperback (6x9) - $15.00

Have you always had a burning desire to own a business? Have you ever thought, "I'd like to be a businessperson... but can I do it successfully and still hold fast to my Christian values?" Or are you already in business, but wondering how you can make a difference for the kingdom of God? Are you where you want to be in your calling? If any of these questions ring true, then this book is for you! *Biblical Principles for Starting & Operating a Business*, by Patrice Tsague, is an interactive text that will not only help you see business in a different light... it will help you see yourself and God's plan for you in a whole new way. Believe it or not, business was God's idea... and He has provided principles and examples throughout the pages of scripture to show us how it should be done. Take a look... not only was business God's idea... you may find that it is His idea for you!

BIBLICAL ENTREPRENEURSHIP 40-DAY COACHING GUIDE: A Spiritual Journey for Entrepreneurs and Marketplace Believers.

—————————————————————— Paperback (6x9) - $15.00

I dare you to take the 40–Day challenge! Do you spend time studying the Word of God daily and seeking for wisdom concerning your business life? In Mark 1:35, we learn that Jesus got up before daylight to go to a solitary place to pray before starting His day. Jesus understood that if His ministry was to be successful, He could not depend on His natural talents or abilities alone. It was crucial for Him to depend on His relationship with the Father. "...for I always do what pleases Him" (John 8:29). The *Biblical Entrepreneurship 40–Day Coaching Guide* is a tool for entrepreneurs who desire to seek the wisdom of God in various areas of business. It provides patterns of prayer and practical ways to apply the information in their business lives.

TO ORDER ————————————————

Visit **www.nehemiahproject.org** and click on the Online Store tab!